THE WHITE MAN'S
DILEMMA

THE WHITE MAN'S DILEMMA

Climax of the Age of Imperialism

BY

NATHANIEL PEFFER

THE JOHN DAY COMPANY
NEW YORK ~ MCMXXVII

COPYRIGHT, 1927, BY NATHANIEL PEFFER
FIRST PUBLISHED, OCTOBER, 1927

PRINTED IN THE U.S.A.
FOR THE JOHN DAY COMPANY, INC.
BY THE QUINN & BODEN COMPANY, RAHWAY, N. J.

ABOUT THE AUTHOR

NATHANIEL PEFFER was born in New York City in 1890 and taken to Colorado by his family as a child. In 1911 he was graduated from the University of Chicago, where he had begun his journalistic career as editor of the college daily.

After three years of newspaper work in Chicago, he joined the staff of a newspaper in Honolulu. He found Honolulu beautiful but progressive and addicted to modern improvements, so in April, 1915, he left for Shanghai, to work on *The China Press*. A year later he returned to the United States, but was soon on his way back to China, this time to remain four years, first as assistant editor and acting editor of *The China Press*, then in Peking as correspondent of *The New York Tribune* and contributor to a number of American magazines.

Mr. Peffer returned to the United States for the Washington Conference in 1921. The following year he was commissioned by a group of magazines to go to Turkey and Eastern Europe. Since his return to New York in 1924, he has been contributing to various magazines, including *Century, Asia, The New Republic, The Nation* and *The Forum*. In 1926-27 he lectured at the New School for Social Research on imperialism.

In autumn of this year he goes back to China again on a research fellowship granted by the Guggenheim Memorial Foundation.

PREFACE

THIS book is based on a course of lectures given at the New School for Social Research in New York City in the autumn and winter of 1926-27 and now reorganized and rewritten from notes. The writer's object has not been to present a text-book, work of reference or historical treatise. Footnotes, citations of authority, documentation, appendices and the other impedimenta of scholarship are therefore dispensed with; all the demands of modesty do not enjoin the writer, however, from claiming authenticity for his facts. The object of this book has been to analyze a living issue relentlessly flung out at a world already overburdened with issues. Remote as are the materials of which this issue is compounded, it is none the less immediate and vital in its impact on the lives of individual men and women. What could have been more remote than Serajevo or a railroad through Anatolia connecting Berlin and Bagdad? A recent writer has said that if it were not for imperialism, "Mr. Man-in-the-Street would have to go without automobiles because the price of tires and of gasoline would be prohibitive." If that were all, there were small cause for a book or for lamentations. Of the span of the race only an infinitesimal

PREFACE

part has been enriched by the automobile; and men have been happy before, and created civilizations. But there is more. Without imperialism the outward aspects of Mr. Man-in-the-Street's world would be materially altered; also he might be taxed less, and he might be less likely to find his last earthly resting-place on some distant battlefield. The object of this book, then, is to trace the growth of a system, examine its body of ideas, bring out the causes and consequences, and draw the implications to us as nations and individuals. The book is aimed at those who want to understand the forces giving shape to their times, among which none is more decisive than imperialism. Parts of Chapters XII and XIV have appeared in the *Century Magazine* and are reproduced by courtesy of the editors.

NATHANIEL PEFFER

New York City, July, 1927.

CONTENTS

CHAPTER		PAGE
I	*The Issue: An Epoch in Liquidation*	3
II	*Conquistadores, New Style*	20
III	*China: The Classic Example*	33
IV	*The Motives*	66
V	*Backwardness and Riches*	82
VI	*The Results—A World Overrun*	99
VII	*Reaction: The Native Worm Turns*	118
VIII	*Seeds of Discontent*	128
IX	*Seeds of Hatred*	141
X	*Where the Races Meet*	157
XI	*Trumpets of Armageddon*	183
XII	*Efficiency, Progress, Disillusion*	194
XIII	*America Gets Its Stride*	216
XIV	*The Reckoning*	250
XV	*What Might Have Been*	271
XVI	*Conclusion: Dilemma*	287

THE WHITE MAN'S DILEMMA

CHAPTER I

THE ISSUE: AN EPOCH IN LIQUIDATION

I SUPPOSE that underlying all the questions raised in this book is one deeper, broader, more elusive and involving more than politics, diplomacy, economics, militarism and interracial relations. I suppose it is really this: Can human beings ever learn anything from anything? In the light of all history, of recent history in particular, a degree of optimism is implicit in the question. They never did. Yet it is the key question. If it can be answered affirmatively, if, that is, we can learn from experience and profit by the lesson, then every specific question raised in this book can be answered, almost by formula; if it must be answered negatively, then there is no answer to any question here raised, except such as may be given in the event by the operation of a purely mechanistic fatalism.

It can be inferred, then, that no remote and unknown territory will be explored in this book. No recondite facts will be adduced, no esoteric conclusions drawn. The materials presented are open to all who wish to look for them. They are matters of record, even newspaper record. And the conclusions can be drawn by all who are willing to face their possible unpleasantness. In fact, they could never be more obvious than now, when we have just seen them yielded from similar premises. Nor has there ever been a more compelling need that they be faced—in prospect rather than retrospect. For this generation surely cannot endure another lesson such as it has had within ten years; nor, probably, can any other. Yet we are nearer a repetition now than we realize, and it will be inescapable to the generation that follows unless some human agency intervenes; unless, that is, we learn that under unchanging conditions the same causes will always have the same effects.

The subject of this book is imperialism, a loose word loosely used but carrying the clearest of practical meanings. Let imperialism be defined, then, by its meaning in action. The net result of the political history of the last hundred years has been the conquest of nearly all the world by that part of it which lies in western Europe and North America; the conquest of nearly a billion of the non-white and materially backward peoples by the strongest white and most materially advanced nations. Whatever the motives may have been, whatever the methods, however we may differ as to the moral and political issues involved and the advantages and disadvantages to conqueror and conquered, the fact is that practically all of Africa and Asia, all of the insular territories and part of Latin America, are to-day ruled by one

THE ISSUE: AN EPOCH IN LIQUIDATION

or another of the great Powers; if not ruled in full juridical sovereignty, then at least to the degree that their destinies as nations are determined not by themselves but by aliens, and not in their own interests primarily but in the interests of others. This fact, a sheer physical fact, as undisputable as heat and light, is imperialism.

As the net effect of the history of the last hundred years has been the conquest of the non-white peoples by the white, so the outstanding fact of contemporary history is the revolt of the conquered against their conquerors. This, too, is undisputable as a fact, whatever differences there may be as to causes and justification. Its corroboration is to be found on the first pages of our newspapers. The few years since the world war have seen a succession of uprisings in every part of the world. Turkey, Egypt, India, Morocco, Syria, Korea, China, and the Dutch East Indies all have given open, armed challenge to the Powers that dominate them. From other territorial possessions of the Powers, like the Philippines, comes ever more insistently the demand for independence. On the American continent Mexico, Nicaragua, Haiti and Santo Domingo, with the moral support of all Latin America, make ever more vigorous protests against the encroachments of the United States. These movements may take one form or another. They may be actual organized revolts, sporadic outbreaks, mass demonstrations, or only inarticulate but widespread disaffection. But whatever their outward manifestation, they have an inner unity. Not only have they common motive—unwillingness to remain subject to an alien state—and a common objective—to win their independence—but they have the same roots and are watered from the same springs, as we shall see. And for us of the ruling nations they have the same results: diplomatic notes, warnings, gunboats to emphasize warnings, troops to back up warnings, limited occupations to "protect life and property," and ultimately interventions in force, if not war.

As the outstanding fact of contemporary history is the revolt of the conquered peoples against their conquerors, so the history of the next few decades will turn on the settlement of this conflict. That it must be settled is clear from all the internal evidence, as well as from the deductions to be drawn from a sense of history. It may be postponed, given a great deal of wisdom, insight and imagination on the part of our governments, more than we have any reason to expect from governments. But it cannot be permanently evaded. Our subject nationalities want to be free and mean to win their freedom, by force if necessary. We on our part manifestly do not want to release them. We must, then, either persuade them to renounce their aspiration, prevent them from attempting to achieve it by their own strength, or interpose greater strength against them. And this

THE ISSUE: AN EPOCH IN LIQUIDATION

is the stuff of international relations of the not distant future, to a certain extent of the international politics of to-day.

Thus we complete the cycle which began in the middle of the last century: first the expansion of the powerful states of Europe and the subjugation of weak and materially undeveloped lands; then the struggle among the conquerors over the most desirable spoils, culminating in at least two major wars; and now back to the first stage, that of having to conquer the weak and undeveloped lands, with the difference now that they are neither so weak nor so undeveloped, nor so unconscious of their power of resistance. The issue to-day is not so much which nation shall have the prizes as whether there are to be any prizes at all.

The conflict just outlined I wish to deal with from a point of view not usually taken in public discussions. In practice there are only two approaches to the subject, the liberal and the conservative. Both are oversimplified, both are unreal, and both have the characteristics of most political controversy in that the division is on considerations neither vital nor pertinent to the subject. In fact, the one is not conservative, the other not liberal, except as those adjectives are technical political descriptions.

The conservative says in effect: We have vested interests in China and India and Nicaragua and Mexico and other backward countries, and they must be protected. These countries cannot govern themselves without revolutions, maintain law and order, guarantee the uninterrupted security of our capital and make accessible their natural resources for which we have need. Our governments therefore must intervene to protect our legal rights whenever threatened; and in the end it is better to take the backward countries over altogether and give them the benefits of good government and roads and schools and sewer systems and economic development and a little civilization generally. It is for their own good as well as ours. The liberal says we "ought" not. We ought not to mistreat the backward peoples but give them a helping hand. We do not need to control them for our material advantage. And they themselves will get along better if we only let them alone. In short, we ought to take the more idealistic course. And so the controversy proceeds, with those as the alternatives. Why should we be altruistic about Nicaragua or China or the Philippines or India and sacrifice our business interests to impractical idealism? Or, why should we not?

But these are not the alternatives. If they were there would be nothing to discuss. Twenty years ago, even ten, we could permit ourselves the luxury of academically debating whether we should be more generous to those over whom we had power; and if we decided not to, as of course we always did, no penalty was attached. Indeed, we could lay unction to ourselves for having been broad enough to consider it. But the question now is not whether we should be more generous, but whether or not we have to do under compulsion that which we distantly considered doing out of magnanimity. The question is no longer, is it right to rule other nations as we like, but can we? Of what use to debate whether we should make concessions to China and whether China is advanced enough to be allowed to fix its own tariff, when Chinese troops have driven us out of all but the ports lying under our naval guns?

The moral aspects of imperialism will be ignored in this book. Whether it is right or wrong will be taken as a question apart and extraneous to the issue. For one thing, what does it matter? Suppose imperialism is wrong. Suppose it can be demonstrated to be morally indefensible. What evidence is there in history or contemporary relations on which to believe that that would make any appreciable difference in action? There are individuals, even groups, responsive to the claims of abstract idealism and willing to make it the criterion of their conduct. They are many, but in proportion to the mass they are a helpless minority, and in influence at the centers of power they are negligible, even relative to their number. Men collectively act only in obedience to the dictates of their material interest, or what they believe to be their material interest. This is not said invidiously. There is no reason why they should not. There may be good reason why they should.

The value of conscious idealism as a working motive in human conduct, especially as between groups, may be questioned. Generously inspired though they may be, gratuitous and unrequited benefactions inevitably lay up a claim for gratitude. And situations inevitably arise when the claim is presented. The net result to the recipient usually is loss. He may not have wanted what was given to him gratuitously, he may need what is demanded of him in return. Also the consciousness of having conferred benefit is too likely to be taken as excuse for a fall from grace and self-service. And since we ourselves draw the balance as between benefaction and self-service, it is only natural to overweigh the benefaction. For illustration, consider the contrast between the golden rule as enunciated in the code of Confucius and its Christian version. The Confucian version does not ask of men that they do unto others as they would that others do unto them. It asks only that they do not do unto others as they would not that others do unto them. The distinction is more than verbal. It reflects a deal of mellow race wisdom. Better an attainable code moderately well observed than one unattainable, discouraging, and therefore seldom even aimed at. It is enough to ask of men that they refrain from doing evil, too much to ask that they go about doing good; enough to ask of them justice, too much to ask altruism. Is this negativism? Half the pain of men would be saved by negativism, then. In the present stage of evolution it is doubtful whether men can be trusted to do good to others. For China and India and Egypt and the Philippines and Syria and Java it may be just as well that we shall act toward them as our interests incline us, and that may be enough. In any case it is safe to assume that only thus shall we act, and arguments drawn from morality and appealing to altruism are futile. They will not be made here.

As it happens, they are also unnecessary. Much more forceful arguments can be brought forward, arguments drawn from reality and appealing to the most practical considerations of self-interest. We are confronted with an immediate and inescapable situation. How shall we meet it? We have dependencies which at the least are profitable to us, and at the most are necessary to our economic well-being. They refuse to remain subject to us. Those that have not already defied us give every indication of intention to do so. The only question that need concern us now is what we shall do about it; not what we ought to do but what we can do; and from the point of view wholly and exclusively of our own good.

Can China govern itself? Maybe it can, maybe not; more likely not, as a matter of fact. But, parenthetically, what nation can? The test of capacity for self-government is too often and too complacently applied, especially to others. Moreover, there being no absolute standards of government, whose standards shall be taken as criterion, theirs or ours? And why ours? In any case, all that is irrelevant. The point is that China insists on governing itself without external interference or control, and is manifesting its desires forcibly. And that is the only point that concerns us. For us it is only to decide whether we shall yield and renounce our present rights in China or retain them by force. How China fares under its own government and control must be left to itself, whether for its own good or not.

So, too, will India revert to civil wars and mediæval Asiatic anarchy if the British leave? Maybe it will and maybe not; more likely it will. But the point is that Indian nationalism is becoming more intransigent and it is only a matter of time before the demand for independence will be too strong to be subdued by anything but armed force on the scale of first-class war. And that is the only point that concerns England. For England it is only to decide how it can quell the feeling now surging in India and whether the stake is worth the cost.

And the Philippine Islands: would they go native again if the United States should suddenly, as is hardly likely, redeem its promise to free them? Would they become centers of insurrecto opera bouffe, prey to corruption, misgovernment and economic stagnation? Maybe they would and maybe or another of the great Powers; if not ruled in full juridical sovereignty, then at least to the degree that their destinies as nations are determined not by themselves but by aliens, and not in their own interests primarily but in the interests of others. This fact, a sheer physical fact, as undisputable as heat and light, is imperialism.

As the net effect of the history of the last hundred years has been the conquest of the non-white peoples by the white, so the outstanding fact of contemporary history is the revolt of the conquered against their conquerors. This, too, is undisputable as a fact, whatever differences there may be as to causes and justification. Its corroboration is to be found on the first pages of our newspapers. The few years since the world war have seen a succession of uprisings in every part of the world. Turkey, Egypt, India, Morocco, Syria, Korea, China, and the Dutch East Indies all have given open, armed challenge to the Powers that dominate them. From other territorial possessions of the Powers, like the Philippines, comes ever more insistently the demand for independence. On the American continent Mexico, Nicaragua, Haiti and Santo Domingo, with the moral support of all Latin America, make ever more vigorous protests against the encroachments of the United States. These movements may take one form or another. They may be actual organized revolts, sporadic outbreaks, mass demonstrations, or only inarticulate but widespread disaffection. But whatever their outward manifestation, they have an inner unity. Not only have they common motive—unwillingness to remain subject to an alien state—and a common objective—to win their independence—but they have the same roots and are watered from the same springs, as we shall see. And for us of the ruling nations they have the same results: diplomatic notes, warnings, gunboats to emphasize warnings, troops to back up warnings, limited occupations to "protect life and property," and ultimately interventions in force, if not war.

As the outstanding fact of contemporary history is the revolt of the conquered peoples against their conquerors, so the history of the next few decades will turn on the settlement of this conflict. That it must be settled is clear from all the internal evidence, as well as from the deductions to be drawn from a sense of history. It may be postponed, given a great deal of wisdom, insight and imagination on the part of our governments, more than we have any reason to expect from governments. But it cannot be permanently evaded. Our subject nationalities want to be free and mean to win their freedom, by force if necessary. We on our part manifestly do not want to release them. We must, then, either persuade them to renounce their aspiration, prevent them from attempting to achieve it by their own strength, or interpose greater strength against them. And this is the stuff of international relations of the not distant future, to a certain extent of the international politics of to-day.

Thus we complete the cycle which began in the middle of the last century: first the expansion of the powerful states of Europe and the subjugation of weak and materially undeveloped lands; then the struggle among the conquerors over the most desirable spoils, culminating in at least two major wars; and now back to the first stage, that of having to conquer the weak and undeveloped lands, with the difference now that they are neither so weak nor so undeveloped, nor so unconscious of their power of resistance. The issue to-day is not so much which nation shall have the prizes as whether there are to be any prizes at all.

The conflict just outlined I wish to deal with from a point of view not usually taken in public discussions. In practice there are only two approaches to the subject, the liberal and the conservative. Both are oversimplified, both are unreal, and both have the characteristics of most political controversy in that the division is on considerations neither vital nor pertinent to the subject. In fact, the one is not conservative, the other not liberal, except as those adjectives are technical political descriptions.

The conservative says in effect: We have vested interests in China and India and Nicaragua and Mexico and other backward countries, and they must be protected. These countries cannot govern themselves without revolutions, maintain law and order, guarantee the uninterrupted security of our capital and make accessible their natural resources for which we have need. Our governments therefore must intervene to protect our legal rights whenever threatened; and in the end it is better to take the backward countries over altogether and give them the benefits of good government and roads and schools and sewer systems and economic development and a little civilization generally. It is for their own good as well as ours. The liberal says we "ought" not. We ought not to mistreat the backward peoples but give them a helping hand. We do not need to control them for our material advantage. And they themselves will get along better if we only let them alone. In short, we ought to take the more idealistic course. And so the controversy proceeds, with those as the alternatives. Why should we be altruistic about Nicaragua or China or the Philippines or India and sacrifice our business interests to impractical idealism? Or, why should we not?

But these are not the alternatives. If they were there would be nothing to discuss. Twenty years ago, even ten, we could permit ourselves the luxury of academically debating whether we should be more generous to those over whom we had power; and if we decided not to, as of course we always did, no penalty was attached. Indeed, we could lay unction to ourselves for having been broad enough to consider it. But the question now is not whether we should be more generous, but whether or not we have to do under compulsion that which we distantly considered doing out of magnanimity. The question is no longer, is it right to rule other nations as we like, but can we? Of what use to debate whether we should make concessions to China and whether China is advanced enough to be allowed to fix its own tariff, when Chinese troops have driven us out of all but the ports lying under our naval guns?

The moral aspects of imperialism will be ignored in this book. Whether it is right or wrong will be taken as a question apart and extraneous to the issue. For one thing, what does it matter? Suppose imperialism is wrong. Suppose it can be demonstrated to be morally indefensible. What evidence is there in history or contemporary relations on which to believe that that would make any appreciable difference in action? There are individuals, even groups, responsive to the claims of abstract idealism and willing to make it the criterion of their conduct. They are many, but in proportion to the mass they are a helpless minority, and in influence at the centers of power they are negligible, even relative to their number. Men collectively act only in obedience to the dictates of their material interest, or what they believe to be their material interest. This is not said invidiously. There is no reason why they should not. There may be good reason why they should.

The value of conscious idealism as a working motive in human conduct, especially as between groups, may be questioned. Generously inspired though they may be, gratuitous and unrequited benefactions inevitably lay up a claim for gratitude. And situations inevitably arise when the claim is presented. The net result to the recipient usually is loss. He may not have wanted what was given to him gratuitously, he may need what is demanded of him in return. Also the consciousness of having conferred benefit is too likely to be taken as excuse for a fall from grace and self-service. And since we ourselves draw the balance as between benefaction and self-service, it is only natural to overweigh the benefaction. For illustration, consider the contrast between the golden rule as enunciated in the code of Confucius and its Christian version. The Confucian version does not ask of men that they do unto others as they would that others do unto them. It asks only that they do not do unto others as they would not that others do unto them. The distinction is more than verbal. It reflects a deal of mellow race wisdom. Better an attainable code moderately well observed than one unattainable, discouraging, and therefore seldom even aimed at. It is enough to ask of men that they refrain from doing evil, too much to ask that they go about doing good; enough to ask of them justice, too much to ask altruism. Is this negativism? Half the pain of men would be saved by negativism, then. In the present stage of evolution it is doubtful whether men can be trusted to do good to others. For China and India and Egypt and the Philippines and Syria and Java it may be just as well that we shall act toward them as our interests incline us, and that may be enough. In any case it is safe to assume that only thus shall we act, and arguments drawn from morality and appealing to altruism are futile. They will not be made here.

As it happens, they are also unnecessary. Much more forceful arguments can be brought forward, arguments drawn from reality and appealing to the most practical considerations of self-interest. We are confronted with an immediate and inescapable situation. How shall we meet it? We have dependencies which at the least are profitable to us, and at the most are necessary to our economic well-being. They refuse to remain subject to us. Those that have not already defied us give every indication of intention to do so. The only question that need concern us now is what we shall do about it; not what we ought to do but what we can do; and from the point of view wholly and exclusively of our own good.

Can China govern itself? Maybe it can, maybe not; more likely not, as a matter of fact. But, parenthetically, what nation can? The test of capacity for self-government is too often and too complacently applied, especially to others. Moreover, there being no absolute standards of government, whose standards shall be taken as criterion, theirs or ours? And why ours? In any case, all that is irrelevant. The point is that China insists on governing itself without external interference or control, and is manifesting its desires forcibly. And that is the only point that concerns us. For us it is only to decide whether we shall yield and renounce our present rights in China or retain them by force. How China fares under its own government and control must be left to itself, whether for its own good or not.

So, too, will India revert to civil wars and mediæval Asiatic anarchy if the British leave? Maybe it will and maybe not; more likely it will. But the point is that Indian nationalism is becoming more intransigent and it is only a matter of time before the demand for independence will be too strong to be subdued by anything but armed force on the scale of first-class war. And that is the only point that concerns England. For England it is only to decide how it can quell the feeling now surging in India and whether the stake is worth the cost.

And the Philippine Islands: would they go native again if the United States should suddenly, as is hardly likely, redeem its promise to free them? Would they become centers of insurrecto opera bouffe, prey to corruption, misgovernment and economic stagnation? Maybe they would and maybe not; that there would be marked retrogression for a time is hardly to be doubted. But even so, the point is that Filipino sentiment for independence is universal and sharpening. It may or may not be mistaken, it may or may not be regrettable, even from the point of view of the Filipinos' welfare and regarded with the greatest detachment; but it exists, and that is all that matters for practical purposes. And the time will come when for the United States the only logical question will be whether retaining the Philippines is worth repeating the experience of England in Ireland.

Who can doubt that the Egyptian peasant enjoyed greater security, more equitable taxation, and other material benefits after the British occupation? Or that the native of Haiti is better off for having roads, and prevention of disease, and for being exempt from periodic revolutions into which he is kidnapped to fight for he knows not what general? Or that Nicaragua will be a safer, more orderly, more prosperous country, now that it is being absorbed by the United States?

Still more important, will our vested interests be secure in backward countries freed from foreign control, whether at our volition or by their own efforts? That can be answered summarily. They will not. Taking as our standard of good government the one laid down by the late Governor General Wood in the Philippines, namely, a government under which foreign capital can be invested with security—which is the standard we do adopt in practice—then the backward regions now dominated by us are not capable of setting up good governments at present and our investments would not be safe. They know neither the concept nor the technique of due process of law. They neither set any high value upon stability nor do they know how to maintain it. They cannot practise social efficiency, nor do they regard it as a good. Turn back the foreign concessions and settlements in China to the Chinese, and within a year public services of all kinds will have run down; taxation will be determined by caprice, favor or the highest bribe; inefficiency will clog every public activity and property values will decline; and most private activities, the multitude of foreign interests built up over generations, will suffer disastrously if not beyond recovery. It need not be said also that the oil of Mesopotamia, the rubber of Sumatra, the iron of China, and the palm oil of the African Congo cannot be made available for the world's use without continued foreign control.

The vast number and variety of raw materials which are indispensable to the functioning of our industrial machinery, and so many of which are found in economically undeveloped and foreign-controlled lands, cannot be obtained expeditiously, cheaply and profitably if these lands are freed from foreign control. Their inhabitants, whether primitive like the

THE ISSUE: AN EPOCH IN LIQUIDATION

Central Africans or civilized like the Chinese and Hindus, have not the experience, technology and organizing efficiency to develop their own resources on the scale demanded by modern industry. They cannot do so without foreign supervision and capital. But foreign capital cannot be invested in such regions without a measure of political control and almost complete financial control; otherwise it would be wasted by inefficiency if not eaten away by corruption. In short, let the dependencies of the great empires go free, and not only should we lose economically but our whole industrial system would be thrown out of joint.

All this may be true. But what if it is? It does not solve the issue or dispose of the issue, it only states it. Granted that the subject peoples are not what is called "ready for independence", whatever that may mean; granted that they themselves will fare worse if left to themselves; granted that we stand to lose heavily if they are freed of our control. The issue nevertheless is this: Do they demand their freedom, and if so can we help giving it to them; if we can, how and at what cost, and what is the relation between the cost and what we lose if they regain their freedom? And this is the only issue, notwithstanding that it is never touched on by our public men, our public prints, our "big business men", and our so-called experts—for the reason, I suppose, that what are known as practical men cannot be expected to approach with common sense any of the simpler, more obvious facts of everyday reality or even to recognize them until their make-believe world tumbles about their ears in wars, economic crashes or class conflicts. It is our practical men, indeed, who have talked the most elaborate nonsense about our colonies and protectorates "first setting their house in order" (in which case they would not have to tolerate us any longer, so we obstruct them when they try to set their house in order), and letting us develop their resources for them (though we get the resources developed), and learning prosperity under our guidance and tutelage (though the profits go to us). And it is they, strangely, and not our liberals, professional reformers and utopians, who evolved the concept expressed in that matchless locution, the white man's burden. To be sure, with many of them it is rationalization of their desires or just hypocrisy, but not, I am afraid, with most. Most of them, I am afraid, really believe it. Therein lies the danger.

At any rate, that is the issue with which this book is concerned. And I want to deal with it truly practically, that is, as something that must be acted upon. I want to discuss it as a concrete, fundamental question of national polity. I do not mean a question in the usual connotations of "international relations," "foreign affairs," treaties, alliances, balance of power, protocols, etc., out of the patois of experts. I mean

THE ISSUE: AN EPOCH IN LIQUIDATION

a concrete question involving our economic status, our social forms and our everyday welfare as individuals. As a matter of fact, do not even the artificialities of the world of diplomats and bureaucrats affect us as individuals intimately enough? Who of us in this generation can say that his life has not been differently cast, if not warped, by the war of 1914-1918?

Imperialism and its present consequences are not of artificial origin and growth, although much may have been grafted on to them. It may be true that England acquired an empire in a fit of absent-mindedness, as America appears to be acquiring one now in a fit of idealism. It may also be true that China and India and Syria and Nicaragua are being seduced from proper appreciation of the benefits of foreign idealism by the Moscow Antichrist. But these are only half-truths. More than charming vagaries have inspired conquest, more than satanism revolt. Both in fact are products of the forces of their time. The discoveries of science and their application to economic processes gave the Occident range and command of weapons that made conquest of the rest of the world possible. Industrialization gave it needs that made conquest essential if not inevitable. Simultaneously the French and American Revolutions, or the causes of which they were effects, generated the ideas of nationalism and democracy. These ideas, disseminated by the new means of communication and by our own proselyting, and then intensified by the world war, have produced the present ferment in the subject nations and made revolt inevitable. Both—conquest and revolt alike—are the results of the operation of a ruthless, irresistible logic of history.

So also is the pass we now find ourselves in logical and inevitable. What remains to be determined is whether conflict also is inevitable. To avoid it is far from easy. The pass seems closed at both ends. On the one side our social economy is bound up with our territorial possessions. We have large vested interests in them, and we need them for natural resources to feed our industrial machinery and as markets to take the products of our industrial machinery. We have a moral vested interest in our possessions in so far as we have overconvinced ourselves that our honor is bound up with keeping the flag flying wherever we have once unfurled it. On the other side, to retain our territorial possessions may require an expenditure of men, money and energy in the form of military force that may so severely strain us as also to require an enormous and complicated social and economic readjustment, perhaps as serious a one as would result from the loss of empire.

Which shall it be? It must be one or the other, and the longer we postpone decision or refuse to face the necessity of choice, the more restricted is our freedom of choice. We may then in fact have

THE ISSUE: AN EPOCH IN LIQUIDATION

to do both. By unwillingness or inability to face the necessity of decision with regard to China, we are already on the border of catastrophe. Sooner or later we shall be brought there in every other region similarly controlled. Whatever chance there is of a way out with minimum of loss is by way of foreseeing consequences and anticipating them. So far we have made no effort to do so. We are unwilling or unable to see even what is involved and what are the factors entering into the decision. The question —Which?—and the factors entering into the question constitute the subject of this book.

CHAPTER II

CONQUISTADORES, NEW STYLE

A WORD must be said about this matter of conquest. It must be seen in proper perspective. The temptation is great to make moral judgments; but morality is relative. About the history of the era of imperialism there is, to be sure, an atmosphere somewhat miasmic. The doings of the European Powers in Africa and Asia throughout the nineteenth century and early in the twentieth make strong reading for the squeamish. Similar conduct in private life, measured by the standards commonly set for individuals, is repaid by ostracism if not by compulsory isolation.

It is impossible to read the most objective factual account of the white man's aggressions in the last hundred years without being stirred to righteous indignation and concluding that he is a barbarian; but it is wiser to bear in mind the long procession of history and to be philosophical. This is no new phenomenon in history. The human animal has gone preying before, in fact he always has. And the sway of man over man has never been exercised very gently. It is natural and proper for anyone with a sense of justice and an aspiration toward decency in human relations to be incensed over the English in

India and China, the Russians in Persia, the Italians in Abyssinia, the French in Tunis, the English and French and Germans and Belgians and Italians everywhere in Africa and the Americans in the Philippines; but it is necessary to remember that others have done likewise before and with no more delicacy and restraint. The white man in his days of might has been no more aggressive than the strong races that have preceded him in supremacy. He has been no more predacious or cruel or destructive than the Mongols, Huns, Tartars and Goths who ravaged Europe and Asia in the thousand years that went before. The hordes led by Jenghis Khan, systematically laying waste where they set foot, slaying whom they met, and leaving catacombs behind them across two continents, were worse. So were others.

What is new in this latter phase, what distinguishes the latter-day conquistador from his predecessors, is that the white man has reduced predacity to a system, given it a methodology, a philosophy, a conscious social motive and a moral justification—the white man's burden. Tribes, nations and races have gone marauding always, either driven in mass movements by we know not what inner need or impulse, or led by some masterful personality, some individual of indomitable will and the ambition to bend the world to his whim, an Attila, a Jenghis Khan, a Timurlane. And the weak who lay in their path have been cut down or put under the yoke. But the passions are spent and the lust for slaying slaked with killing enough, or the tyrant dies. The wave is broken and recedes; the conquerors are driven back or are absorbed and disappear from history. A system, however, needs no passion for stimulus, depends on no masterful individual. It goes on without end of its own drive and momentum—unless, that is, a period is put to the epoch of which it is part.

The West has not only institutionalized conquest, but subtilized it. In an older, simpler, and more unsophisticated day when we went out to impose our will on another country, we sent armies to overrun it and reduce it to submission. Then we established our garrisons, took over the government, and ruled the country for our purposes. Later, when the advances of science had already made life a little more complex, we had only to dispatch gunboats, shell ports and occupy strategic centers from which we could overshadow the country without having to occupy all of it. Our ships were fast and could move troops more expeditiously, our guns reached further and were more deadly. But in an age of progress these crude and primitive methods have long since been abandoned.

You no longer occupy ports and maintain distant expeditions. It is too hard and too costly, unless the country is small and not too far away. Also it is a little too flagrantly immoral and your own liberal and humanitarian elements protest too much. And too many professions of international friendship and idealism stand on the record to constrain you to the semblance of decorum. So you proceed with more indirection and subtlety, and, as it turns out, with greater profit.

You send your representatives to the country which attracts your aspirations. They cultivate a knowledge of local conditions and the acquaintance and good will of the native ruler, if it is an autocratically ruled country, or of the cabinet ministers if it has the outward forms of modern government. The native ruler may have expensive tastes in concubines and palaces and new toys like automobiles with gold and glittering ornaments; native rulers usually do. Or the cabinet ministers may have similar tastes, or their political groups may have ambitions which cannot prosper without financial aid. The natural limits to revenue from taxation in such countries, since they are economically undeveloped, do not provide a surplus for lavish personal tastes or subsidy for political maneuvers. In fact, a large part of the revenue is already devoted to those ends, without formality of budget.

Your representatives—they need not be official and diplomatic representatives, but just enterprising citizens with the backing of industrial and banking groups—are well aware of these circumstances. They are also well aware that the country has valuable deposits of iron or gold or diamonds or copper or oil. It becomes a matter then merely of combining circumstances which are in their nature complementary. It is a matter of a few discreet calls, a few polite conversations in which no sordid details are intruded, for gentlemen understand each other in these affairs. Prompted by the mutual friendship which has traditionally linked the two countries, you make a loan of $10,000,000—or £2,000,000 or 50,000,000 francs or 40,000,000 marks. In return you have the exclusive right to exploit the gold mines or diamond mines or iron fields or coal mines or oil wells, whichever they happen to be. You get what is technically known as a concession. The native ruler gets the means to indulge his newest concubine's whim or acquire another concubine; or the cabinet minister gets the means to further his intrigue against the rival clique.

But mines are not enough. You must have the means of bringing their products out to market. You must have a railroad. It is a logical sequence then to get a concession to build the railroad in exchange for another loan. It is a logical sequence for you, and it is equally logical for the native ruler or his ministers. Their personal share of the first loan, though not small, is already exhausted in satisfying personal tastes or political ambitions. And appetite comes while eating. The railroad is built, and you bring your diamonds or gold or copper or oil to the ports. But the ships which are to carry the mine products from the ports to the world markets must have harbors. You construct a harbor. Also you must have an agency for handling the large sums of money involved, making credit arrangements and carrying out the complicated processes of international exchange. You start a bank. You must insure your properties and incidentally other properties like yours. You start an insurance company. You bring out numerous employes from your own country for the more skilled and responsible duties. They must be provided with the necessities to which they are accustomed, so numerous shopkeepers, wholesale agents and the like come with them, and later doctors, lawyers and other professional men. These must live with an approximation, at least, to the manner in which they have been accustomed at home. They build their houses in their own architectural style, lay out streets, install electric lights and some of the sanitary conveniences, organize clubs and take up ground for parks and baseball diamonds and cricket fields. You have in effect your own community, set in the midst of an alien land. A community like this must have a medium of communication of information and an organ for the dissemination of its own point of view. You start a newspaper. Also it must have an orderly and efficient administration of communal affairs, and an administration of justice according to laws and traditions to which its inhabitants are accustomed. You have then a self-sufficient and autonomous community. All these activities bring out more people from home and lead to the establishment of more activities, and to the making of more loans and the acquisition of more concessions.

How are the loans repaid? Usually with more loans and the concessions that go with loans. The proceeds of the first loans having been squandered, as they usually are and as it was expected that they would be, and no more sources of revenue being open to the native government than before, the native government is in default. What happens in such circumstances? One forecloses on the mortgage, or makes another loan to cover the first one and gets another concession for security. Thus the native government is ever tempted to incur debts it never can repay, and both loans and concessions are pyramided. A whole chain of logical sequences has been linked together, all legal, correct, and in the best usage. But what is left to the native rulers and his ministers except their concubines and their lavish tastes and their personal ambitions? They still rule, but what? You have not conquered the country. It is still a sovereign state, with a king and a parliament and ministries and laws. You only own the means whereby it lives. And that is enough. Let me own or control a country's natural resources, banks, and means of communication, and I care not who sits in its parliament and makes its laws. The country is mine.

I have perhaps oversimplified the whole process.

I have assumed, for instance, that there is only one "you." If that were so, much of recent history would be written differently. As a matter of fact, there are many—a British you, a French, a German, an Italian, a Belgian, a Japanese. (I omit the Russian purposely, for he is in another catagory. When a Briton or an American alienates a railway in another country or takes over the collection of its customs revenues, that is legitimate enterprise, and constructive, and even for the other country's good; when a Russian does the same, it is diabolical and subversive of the other country. The distinction must be apparent to all who are not themselves wrong-minded.) And the mine which the British want, the Americans and French also want and try to get. Sometimes one of them gets one mine and all that follows from it, while the others get still other mines and all that follows. In that case we have what are technically known as spheres of influence, each Power having monopolistic rights in its own sphere and incidentally maneuvering to encroach on every other sphere. If there is no such division into spheres, because the native ruler and his ministry are too amenable to the persuasion of, say, the British, the others may find it convenient and possible to change the ruler or his ministry. This can be done by providing the sinews of war for an opposition party. Constitutional methods are preferable, but revolutions are always effective. Then the Briton retaliates in kind, restoring those who have the proper point of view. And thus may be explained so much of what is known as chaos in backward countries that cannot maintain law and order and are always embroiled in revolutions.

Indeed, revolutions are not without their uses. For one's mines and banks and buildings cannot be jeopardized by disorder, and one must on such occasions call on one's government. It is on such occasions that there occurs the landing of marines and other military forces for what is technically known as protecting the life and property of a nation's citizens. Since disorders may be expected not infrequently, as we have seen, it may become necessary for the marines and other military forces to remain permanently for the protection of life and property. There have been in fact few instances where it was ever again deemed safe for the occupying forces to leave. The competition for the sympathy and support of the native government and the possession of the most desirable concessions may lead to nothing more serious than periodic overturning of the government and occasional revolutions. But more often it engenders an atmosphere of diplomatic intriguery and international rancors. And the last link in the chain of logical sequences we have seen forged is quite likely to be war.

The principle of methodology remains unaffected, however. Imperialism can now be waged without bombarding navies and armies of occupation. It can be waged by loans and concessions; the bond is mightier than the sword. It can and now is being waged even more subtly—by implanting influences. Missionaries, education, industrialism and modern conveniences are equally potent with loans and concessions. You send ten missionaries and two business men to a Chinese or Hindu or Persian or Arabian village; ten to two is about the usual proportion in the beginning. They establish themselves in their own quarters or compounds, in which they reproduce their native Bloomsbury or Grand Rapids atmosphere as nearly as possible. They bring with them soap and folding bathtubs and oil lamps and domestic conveniences and hot-water bags and medicines and straw hats and chewing gum (Mr. Wrigley's confections are not unknown in this year of progress on the Tibetan borders). And the Chinese or Persians who come to the foreigners' households as servants, or sell them the grain for their porridge, or live next door, or work in the business men's offices, or attend the missionaries' school, observe the new and tempting and usually more efficient devices. They gradually acquire a taste for such devices. The taste becomes a demand; a demand which the foreigner alone can satisfy, and the satisfaction of which forms new habits and makes a new way of life, the foreigner's way of life.

When a large enough proportion of the population has acquired the demands, an economic dependence on the foreigner has been established and hostages have been given. From the first cake of soap in the native village to need for a railroad which can be built only by the foreigner with the accompaniment of foreign economic and then political ascendancy, is not one step but, say, ten. Every foreign compound, though it be isolated one hundred miles from any other white man's residence and though its purpose be the teaching of the Sermon on the Mount or the cure of leprosy, is an instrument for undermining native independence. Shanghai and Bombay, Bagdad and Teheran, with their automobiles and electric lights and elevators and steam cranes, all of which the natives have come to regard as necessities, have been subjugated in effect if not in international law. They have been subjugated culturally. What follows is only a corollary. In large part the reaction against the white man wherever he has established his dominion may be attributed to protest, if only unconscious, against the destruction of a civilization which is the accumulation of a race's achievements and the concentrate of its memories. And much of the disintegration now visible in certain parts of the world is the consequence of the disquilibrium and inevitable conflict when two civilizations inherently irreconcilable are flung against each other without preparation or opportunity for slow mutual adjustment, if adjustment be possible. The twentieth century and the first century after Christ are being lived simultaneously. The result is not only lack of inner harmony, but revolt of what is indigenous and interwoven with the spirit of a people against what is alien and superimposed.

We have come a long way, then, from the early Portuguese, Dutch and Spanish adventurers who went forth to reduce a realm for their liege lords; a long way from the days of the gunboat squadrons that steamed into distant ports, terrified the natives with a few salvos, and landed officers to dictate treaties acknowledging the "protection" of the nation which despatched the gunboats; a long way from the pioneer bands which set out for newly discovered lands to found a new home. We have come furthest from the latter. What is there in common between the English who landed on the stern and rockbound coast of Massachusetts, and the English now in Burma and Hongkong—or the descendants of the English in Manila and Port au Prince, Haiti? What is there in common between colonial settlements in primitive and sparsely populated regions and the communities of foreign traders in India, Mesopotamia, Syria and the Philippines?

Colonists take up primeval land with intent to establish there a branch of their own civilization. They bring with them their families and their goods, their language, traditions, habits and culture. They expect to remain, to identify themselves with the soil and to root their posterity there. The English or French or Americans in India or China or North Africa or the Philippines go for some definite purpose of exploitation, and identify themselves with the land they are in only so far as is necessary for purposes of exploitation. They live, in fact, wholly insulated from the life about them. And when their object has been achieved, when, that is, they have made money enough, they go home. They are transient agents of home offices. Hongkong, Singapore and the Philippines are not colonies as Virginia, Australia and Canada were. They are autonomous trading posts.

The day of colonialism is long gone. Imperialism is something vastly different. It does not even denote empire any more. We do not take over sovereignty, assume the functions of government and impose our own laws. We control only to the point necessary to obtain that for which we have come. We set up whatever régime enables us most satisfactorily to carry out the exploitation we find most profitable. This control can be won without force of arms and maintained without garrisons. It is an economic conquest only. But for the conquered it is no less a yoke for being wrought of gold.

CHAPTER III

CHINA: THE CLASSIC EXAMPLE

WE have been discussing imperialism thus far in the general and abstract. I want now to go to the other extreme and take it in its most concrete form. I want to take one specific case of imperialism, so that we may see its development, anatomy, and manner of functioning. The perfect illustration, the very model, is of course China. Every element in every other imperialistic situation is to be found in China, every force at work everywhere else is working in China, every effect caused by the aggressions of the strong white Powers on weak, non-white nations is being felt in China and by the Powers having relations with China. There the whole circle is described, from the groping, half-accidental, almost unconscious beginnings to the present climax, with peremptory demands by China, foreign reluctance to yield and inability to yield without serious loss, foreign residents in China virtually in a state of siege with military and naval expeditions being rushed to their protection, and the shadow of war ever more menacing. China, moreover, is not only the biggest stake in the imperialistic game but its severest test. As it will be with China, so eventually it will be with all Asia. And if Asia is lost, then ultimately the whole imperialistic game is lost and the liquidation of an epoch has set in.

In point of continuity of national identity and culture China is the oldest of the nations of to-day which are accounted great. Its written chronicles run back twenty-five hundred years, legendary or only partly authenticated accounts go back twenty-five hundred more. The Chinese were a civilized people when, as they sometimes like to remind us, our own ancestors were painting themselves blue and purple. That may be neither anthropologically nor historically quite correct, but the comparison implied is not so much overdrawn. At any rate, most of Europe was a wilderness populated by savage and semi-savage tribes when the Chinese already had an organized society, an elaborated system of government, religion, philosophy, traditions, arts, mechanical inventions, and refinements of social intercourse. Before William the Conqueror had set foot in England, China was already a world state.

China had had foreign relations long before European warships pounded its gates open. The common belief that it had lived in hermit isolation is erroneous. Chinese silks were worn by the fashionables of imperial Rome, Chinese traders penetrated all of Asia and exchanged goods with Egypt, and Arab and Indian traders were bringing their wares to Canton not long after the time of Jesus. Persian religious

CHINA: THE CLASSIC EXAMPLE

refugees, Nestorian Christians fleeing from religious persecution, and Moslem converts made their way to China in the period that was Europe's dark age. They were welcomed. In the thirteenth century Marco Polo the Venetian came to China with his father and his uncle. They were foreign, white, alien in appearance and costume, in language and manners and ideas, and they came uninvited. Yet not only were they not treated on the Anglo-Saxon formula, "Look 'ere 'Arry, there goes a foreigner, let's 'eave a brick at 'im," but Marco Polo was taken into the government, and before he left China had served as governor of the important trading center of Yangchow. And he returned to Venice to thrill his compatriots with his reports of the great wealth and culture of China, the efficiency and orderliness of its government, the magnificence of its cities, and the general superiority of its people.

Toward the end of the sixteenth century the first Jesuits arrived in order to propagate Christianity. They were permitted to remain and do so. Even more, they were given special protection and accorded honors by the court because of the scientific learning they brought with them. The astronomical observatory they erected still stands along the East Wall in Peking. The Jesuits were followed by members of other Christian orders, the Dominicans and Franciscans, who forthwith and in the best European manner fell to quarreling over theological interpretations. How to translate into Chinese the word for God was the cause of one dispute; whether to allow Chinese converts to continue their ancestor worship was another. Their wrangling, which began to take on political aspects, eventually brought them under suspicion and resulted in a certain amount of restriction, but on the whole they were permitted to carry on their religious work under conditions of complete tolerance. More, indeed, than they find in 1927 in Mississippi and Arkansas, and certainly more than there was in Europe at the time. In the seventeenth century, it must be remembered, the only parts of the world where a Christian could feel reasonably safe from being disemboweled by another Christian in the name of Christianity were those parts populated and ruled over by infidels like the Turks and heathen like the Chinese. It is unnecessary to recite religious ceremonies like the Inquisition and St. Bartholomew's Night.

It may have been this lapse from a proper valuation of the things of the spirit that fired European zeal to convert the heathen parts, especially China. Even now missionaries commonly hold it in derogation of the Chinese that they do not, as it is said, take a spiritual attitude toward religion, do not feel deeply enough about it. That is true. They do not. They never have considered religion to be of such momentous concern as to kill one another over it or even to make one another's lives miserable. One of their distinguishing characteristics, indeed, has always been religious tolerance. Buddhist, Taoist, Mohammedan, Jew, Catholic, Episcopalian, Baptist, Holy Roller, rationalist and skeptic have dwelt side by side in amity, indifferent to each other's religious beliefs. To each individual has been left the right to determine and express his relation to the universe as befitted his temperament, that being his private affair. The Chinese, significantly, are the only race to have completely assimilated the Jew. The Jewish colony that came to Honan is now absorbed, and sense even of Jewish identity has been lost. In result, the Chinese have escaped the horrors of religious bitterness and been spared Europe's periodic bloodbaths in the name of God.

Missionaries were not, however, the only emissaries from Europe. The explorers who found the Eastern passage were followed by traders and adventurers, stopping first in India and then making their way around the whole coast of Asia. They gave dubious representation of their race and civilization. They were, indeed, pestilential. All the evidence bears out the verdict of St. Francis Xavier, whose letter describing the atmosphere of a Portuguese settlement on the Indian coast is quoted by Henry M. Hyndman in "The Awakening of Asia." St. Francis arrived in India in 1542 and later started for China, his real goal, but died within sight of its shores.

"There is a power here," he wrote, "which I

may call irresistible, to thrust men headlong into the abyss, where besides the seductions of gain and the easy opportunities of plunder their appetites for greed will be sharpened by having tasted it, and there will be a whole torrent of low examples and evil customs to overwhelm and sweep them away. Robbery is so public and so common that it hurts no one's character and is hardly a fault. . . . Everywhere and at all times it is rapine, hoarding and robbery. The devices by which men plunder, the various pretexts under which it is done, who can count? I never cease wondering at the number of new inflections which, in addition to all the usual forms, have been added in this lingo of avarice to the conjugation of that ill-omened verb, 'to rob.' "

The question occurs in passing why, then, St. Francis had to leave his native shores to win men to the teaching of the Nazarene, but as it is a question that may be put as well to the missionary endeavor of the twentieth century there is little point in pursuing it. There appears to be no answer. It is essential, however, to remember that what was apparent to St. Francis Xavier was apparent also to the Asiatics who were its victims, and that they felt even more strongly about the conduct of the Europeans than he did. And the reputation of the Europeans traveled before them.

The first white men to come to China in numbers were the Portuguese who arrived in Canton in 1516-

17. These were well received, but when their compatriots who immediately followed them began to resort to the practices of spoliation which they considered their privilege in the East, they were driven out by order of the Chinese court. But they did manage to establish a few trading settlements here and there on the coast, notably in Macao, the island off Canton. Macao still is a Portuguese possession. Its main industries are opium dens, public gambling houses, and brothels. After the Portuguese came the Dutch. They too were refused permission to remain, but also managed to establish a trading post on the Island of Formosa, though under stringent restrictions. It should be added that they were obstructed by the Portuguese as much as by the Chinese. The Spanish, who already had acquired the Philippines, likewise tried to get a foothold in China, but word of their oppressions in the Philippines, especially their barbarities against Chinese merchants there, had preceded them. They were excluded, Portuguese intrigue again being added to Chinese opposition. The dog-in-the-manger policy among foreigners in China is of ancient lineage. It was born when first there were two foreigners of different nationality in or near the country. If the Chinese have since adopted on their part a policy of playing one foreign Power off against another—as Soviet Russia is being used now against Great Britain—they have only taken a conspicuous cue.

Russia was the first Western Power to succeed in establishing formal relations with China. In 1689 a treaty was concluded fixing the boundaries between the two countries in Manchuria and Siberia, and another was concluded in 1727 permitting a limited number of Russian merchants to come to Peking every three years to trade, and a limited number of Russian missionaries to come for religious proselyting. But Russia was a neighbor and, besides, was itself as much Asiatic as European. Russia's method of approach has always been more astute and understanding, and on the whole more successful.

All this, however, was but the prelude. The real period of contact with the West, that of which we are now witnessing the climax, began in the eighteenth century, when the British East India Company, which had been chartered to trade in India, became interested in the China trade. For back of the British East India Company was England, and England was already mistress of the seas and on the road to world empire politically and commercially. The British trading vessels were followed therefore by men-of-war, and then by official representatives desirous of opening formal and regularized diplomatic and commercial relations with China. Since trade could not be wholly denied, the Emperor Ch'ien Lung by imperial edict set aside Canton as the port of entry for foreign trade. Such trade was not to be carried on by foreigners with China directly, however, but only with a few Chinese firms officially designated as intermediaries—the *co-hongs*, as they were called. Foreign vessels were allowed to put in at the island of Whampoa below Canton and then send their cargoes in small boats to the foreign-owned warehouses outside Canton. The dozen or so Chinese merchants delegated for the purpose took delivery at the factories. They alone had the right to do so, and they alone had the right to sell merchandise to the foreigners, even commodities for their personal needs. And they also were held responsible to the government for all acts committed by the foreigner. The gates of China were still closed, only an aperture had been cut through which the foreigner might be suffered to peep and extend the hand for favors granted him.

So much China would yield but no more, and that was not enough. It was an inconvenient arrangement for the British and an economic handicap, to say nothing of the humiliation. They pressed rigorously for relief. An imposing diplomatic mission was dispatched from London, headed by Lord Macartney, with the object of securing a treaty giving British subjects full commercial rights in China. The mission arrived in 1792 and was accorded lavish hospitality; but there was no treaty. Eleven years later Lord Amherst, former governor-general of India, was sent out with another mission, again without result. Subsequent efforts similarly failed, each one having new humiliations heaped upon it. There was a quality of contemptuous patronage in all Chinese communications addressed to the missions that enraged the British representatives. In word and action the attitude of the Chinese was one of politeness to a supplicant barbarian.

The Chinese were resolved on maintaining their isolation. They wanted no relations with the West, diplomatic, political, or economic. They wanted none of the foreigner at all. Their motives were mixed, arrogance, insularity, and racial conceit entering in as large proportions as caution, fear, and suspicion. But none of these motives was irrational, even such as were abstractly indefensible. It is no doubt unwise for any people to consider itself superior, although all do; and I suppose that no people can be justified, morally and philosophically, in acting toward others as if it were superior, even if it really is. And the Chinese probably were, or at least had better reason for believing so than people usually have. That fact must never be lost sight of. Compared with Ch'ien Lung, George III was a plebeian and vulgarian. The Chinese emperor's sovereignty was acknowledged over a larger area and by more men than could be claimed by any state in Europe. And his realm had been an empire when these upstart intruders were not yet identified in history. Even by those tests which we now apply exclusively, even in "modern improvements" and what is called progress, China

CHINA: THE CLASSIC EXAMPLE

was more advanced than Europe up to the close of the period of which we are talking. Had not Marco Polo, coming from Venice, been awed by the magnificence of the cities he visited in China? The London of Shakespeare, Addison and Dr. Johnson, compared to Peking and Hangchow, was dirty, insanitary, unsafe and badly administered—just "backward." English historians dealing with the period of the negotiations with China may fulminate at China's arrogance, but there was good reason for it. Besides, conceit which is negative and expresses itself only in the desire to be let alone is at the worst a subjective frailty; it is dangerous only when it begets an impulse to impose one's *mores* on others. China, though arrogant, harmed no one, nor had it ever sought to make others over in its own image, by force if necessary and for their good.

So also were China's other grounds for isolation valid. The white man's conduct wherever he had set foot in Asia was not such as to commend his society or add to a feeling of security in those compelled to endure it. The East had had opportunity to learn of the ceaseless wars of Europe. The European nations had made only too clear their disposition to carry their feuds wherever they went, to use their position and influence throughout the East as pawns in the European game and, if necessary, to extend European battlefields to wherever Europeans happened to be. For those not already involved in Europe's dynastic, national, and religious feuds safety lay in keeping all sides at arm's length. And in this the period of aggressive European expansion, that could only mean isolation.

Now it may be that the world is a unity, that the larger interest of the world demands that no part of it be permitted to isolate itself from any other, and that the welfare of mankind is best served by unimpeded movement of men, goods and ideas. But it may also be that every race has the right to determine the question for itself of its own free will. America now claims and exercises the right to exclude whomever it will from its shores, and sets up a tariff which at least restricts the right of others to trade within its boundaries. At any rate, the question was not one of philosophical abstractions for China between, say, 1750 and 1850. It is necessary to ask specifically what demanded entry and what was being excluded by China's policy of isolation. The foreigner, under British leadership, demanded the right to trade, but what he wanted to trade in was opium. Not commerce abstractly but the opium traffic was involved. Or, to the foreigner, it may have been a principle, but the principle turned on opium.

In the popular mind the major associations with the word China are chop suey and opium. Neither is Chinese in origin. Chop suey is indigenous to San Francisco. Opium as a habit-forming drug was brought to China by the white man. The white man

CHINA: THE CLASSIC EXAMPLE

has given the world cheap printing, electricity, railroads and anæsthetics. He has also given it the opium den. While opium was not unknown to the East before the advent of the European, it appears from such scanty evidence as is available that it was first used for smoking by Dutch residents in Java. It was not so used in China, or, if so, then no more than it is in the United States now. It was first brought to China by the Portuguese, but before 1700 only in small quantities. As late as 1729 no more than 200 chests were being imported every year. It was in that year that the Chinese government took official cognizance of the danger of the vice and in an imperial edict proscribed the smoking of opium. But the British East India Company by that time was becoming a power in India. The poppy plant, from which opium is extracted, could be grown in India. The East India Company needed a market. China was the most populous country in the world. The East India Company did save its face morally by forbidding its ships to carry opium to China, but it continued to manufacture opium for exportation to China in other ships—and took the profits, which were handsome. Essentially the opium traffic became a British vested interest—as it still is, though in lesser degree.

The efforts of the Chinese government to curb the evil were fruitless. A loose, decentralized government with a small officialdom in a continental expanse of territory could not prevent consumption once the supply was in the country. And the opening of Canton to the trade and the efforts of smugglers resulted in opium coming into the country in constantly increasing quantities. By 1800 the annual imports had risen to 4,100 chests. In 1797 another imperial edict forbade the importation of opium entirely, but the Chinese government was powerless. Edicts are not enforceable against ships backed by navies. As the supply increased consumption increased, and the habit became rooted. So that they might have a cheaper product, the Chinese began cultivating the poppy themselves. This only served to make the habit more widespread, still more was imported, still more grown at home, and poison was set working through a race. While the Chinese government and the best elements in Chinese life warned, pleaded, expostulated and denounced, the foreigner only answered by demanding the privilege of trading everywhere in China, which merely meant still more opium.

It was in this atmosphere that the controversy over isolation sharpened. The British were more insistent, the Chinese more refractory, and minor conflicts occurred with increasing frequency. The Chinese government at length sent a commissioner to Canton to deal with the situation at first hand. He was the famous Lin Tse-hsü, anti-foreign by instinct and conviction, which is easily understandable, and aggressive by temperament, which resulted in bringing the dispute to a head. After a few years of vain wrangling he resorted to direct action. He confiscated the entire stock of opium in Canton and destroyed it. The British replied as might be expected. They began war, the Opium War, as it is generally called by all except officially-minded historians.

The British won, of course, and in 1842 there was signed the Treaty of Nanking, the document which ended China's isolation, laid the foundations of the subsequent tortuous relations between China and the Western Powers, and formally drew all of Asia into the orbit of Europe. The treaty provided, specifically, the cession to the British of the island of Hongkong, then a barren rock off the southern coast and now one of the world's great ports; the opening to foreign trade of the five ports of Canton, Amoy, Foochow, Ningpo and Shanghai, with land set aside for foreign residence; and an indemnity of $12,000,000 to pay the expenses of the war and $6,000,000 more to pay for the destroyed opium. There were incorporated in the treaty also clauses which subsequently were elaborated to give to the foreign Powers the right to determine China's tariff, and to foreign residents the right of extraterritoriality. Under the latter foreigners are privileged to reside in China immune to Chinese law and taxation, and subject only to the laws of their own country. They can be sued only in their own courts, and for whatever offenses they commit they can be tried only in their own courts, even if the victims be Chinese. Within a few years after the conclusion of the Treaty of Nanking similar treaties were concluded with the other major Powers, the United States being the first to follow Great Britain. These treaties gave all the other Powers the same rights as the British. They included, further, most-favored-nation clauses, whereby all rights or privileges thereafter granted by China to one country were automatically extended to every other country. It was, in short, a famous victory, closing one lofty chapter in history and opening another equally lofty.

There was a treaty of peace, but no peace. More bitter wrangling followed in the next few years in Canton. The foreigners were no better liked for having imposed a humiliating peace, and their presence in a hostile community against its will did not make for harmony. It was inevitable that there should be attacks on foreigners, and there were. Moreover, the Chinese government, its resentment given edge by humiliation, sought to evade fulfillment of the treaty, and being equipped with the Oriental technique of passive resistance, it succeeded fairly well. The Chinese have always been adept at slipping out of their treaty obligations. As an enraged diplomat once exclaimed, "You can't deal with these people, it is like trying to nail jelly on a wall." But all their treaties with the West having been signed under duress, the Chinese in their own eyes have been morally justified. And from any point of view it is difficult to see how morality is involved at all.

A situation which could not endure was broken in 1856, when the Canton authorities seized a small vessel manned by Chinese but flying the British flag because chartered in Hongkong. They ran down the flag and imprisoned the men on the ground that they were pirates and smugglers. There was right and wrong on both sides, legally on Britain's and morally on China's, and under ordinary circumstances the incident could have been settled by routine diplomacy; but against a background of friction it stood as a symbol and there could be only one result. There was war again. This time the French joined the British. They had a pretext. A French missionary had just been killed in the interior. Missionaries, though nuisances to their governments when alive, if killed at the proper time can be an invaluable asset. A missionary indeed is never so useful as when dead. This has reached the dignity of a natural law in all backward regions.

The Anglo-French allies won, of course. Canton was captured, the allied fleet sailed up to Tientsin, eighty miles from Peking, and there another treaty was signed. The foreign Powers won the right to station diplomatic representatives in Peking; the Yangtsze river and more ports were opened to trade;

Kowloon, a strip of territory on the mainland opposite Canton, was ceded to Great Britain, and the status of extraterritoriality was made explicit. There were two other provisions, more significant and enlightening. The importation of opium was legalized. And foreign missionaries were to be allowed to reside anywhere in China, preach the Gospel and give special protection to their converts. The opium den and the Gospel of the Redeemer and Prince of Peace—they had to be taken together and under the compulsion of guns.

Whatever doubts were left in the Chinese mind as to the superiority of the white man and his civilization and the propriety of the propagation of his spiritual concepts were soon resolved. When the Chinese government evaded ratification of the treaty, an Anglo-French expedition marched overland to Peking and took possession of the capital. The court fled but left officials behind to ratify the treaty. The treaty was ratified, but the commanders of the allied expedition determined that it was imperative to teach China a lesson. They sent troops to the Yuan Ming Yuan palace, one of the world's most beautiful edifices and a treasure-house of ancient and irreplaceable objects of art, and deliberately, methodically sacked, looted, and burned it. The lesson was learned. If sometimes Chinese who know history smile a little ironically when they are told, as they so often are, by

CHINA: THE CLASSIC EXAMPLE

experts, diplomats and educators that China's civilization must be reconstructed under Occidental tutelage, the smile must be interpreted in the light of that lesson.

And so the Chinese were cowed. It was plain to them that they could not resist the European. To the European it was plain that the plucking was good, and all varieties of him flocked to the plucking. Thenceforth light was thrown on the contention of officially-minded historians that Europe was interested only in opening China to international intercourse. The Russians came first. They secured a treaty acknowledging their sovereignty over the territory north of the Amur River and including what is now port of Vladivostok. A British diplomatic agent was killed, and an indemnity had to be paid and more ports opened to trade, diplomats coming almost as high as missionaries. France, which had appropriated Cochin China in 1864 by just taking it, in 1874 induced the emperor of Annam, a tributary of China, to accept the status of French protectorate. China protested. There were protracted negotiations, broken by the sending of French troops. They clashed with Chinese troops and war began. It ended in 1885 by Annam and Tongking being recognized as French protectorates, thus giving France all Indo-China. And while China was engaged with France, Great Britain simply occupied Burma, also a tributary of China, and settled down to remain. It did, and in 1894 China had no choice but to recognize Burma's incorporation into the Indian Empire.

Then, curiously, entered Japan, China's tiny neighbor. Japan had been opened to the West out of its isolation of more than two hundred years by the importunities of the United States naval squadron commanded by Commodore Perry in 1853. Japan read the signs of the times quickly. Recognizing that military strength was the only determinant of survival, it set itself quickly and efficiently to the business of modernization and military effectiveness. Partly for this reason and more because the Powers were absorbed in the much bigger game of China, Japan escaped with only minor aggressions from Europe—a few bombardments of its ports, extraterritoriality and the like. But toward the close of the century Japan began to feel its strength and sought to free itself of all restrictions. First it had to demonstrate its right to equality by the only kind of evidence that could convince Europe. And with progress and efficiency and military strength it also began to dream grandiose dreams. Japan would prove to the world that it was as good as any white nation. It, too, could kick China about. It did. A controversy over the status of Korea, historically a dependency of China, was brought to a head, more or less artificially. Japan followed the mode and went to war.

Japan, too, won, and then showed that it had read

the signs of the times too superficially. It forced China to pay a large indemnity, acknowledge the independence of Korea (a euphemism for surrendering Korea to Japanese hegemony) and cede the island of Formosa and the Liaotung peninsula, the southern tip of Manchuria. Possession of the Liaotung peninsula put Peking at the mercy of Japan, and also excluded all Russian prospect of a warm water outlet on the Pacific. No European Power had ventured so much at one fling. There were hurried consultations in Europe, after which Russia, supported by Germany and France, made an official tender of advice to the Japanese government. It was not meet that a victor impose a Punic peace. In the name of the peace of the Far East and as evidence of their traditional friendship, Japan was urged to relinquish the Liaotung peninsula. As an earnest of friendship and the urgency of the advice, Russia moved troops into Siberia. Japan took the advice, relinquished the peninsula, swallowed its chagrin, and made a mental note against the future.

One year later, in 1896, the reward of the righteous was manifested. Russia was granted a concession to build a railway through North Manchuria to connect with the Trans-Siberian Railway. Incidentally it was empowered to exploit mines on both sides of the railway and maintain military guards along the line. That is to say, North Manchuria became Russian. There were again anxious consultations in

Europe, but to the Colossus gratuitous advice could not be tendered so easily.

There was no advice, but the next year two German missionaries were fortuitously and providentially murdered in Shantung, just where the Germans had thought a naval base would be advantageous. There was compensation on the usual scale. Germany was granted a ninety-nine-year lease on Kiaochau Bay, where it proceeded to build itself a naval base, the city of Tsingtau, and a railroad through the heart of Shantung province, besides exploiting mines in the interior. Then was invoked the sacred principle of the balance of power. The essence of this principle in international relations is that no self-respecting country can permit itself to be less voracious than any other, and that when one has grabbed something all others claiming equality must grab as much. Russia therefore demanded and got a twenty-five-year lease on the Liaotung peninsula—that same peninsula—and a concession to build a railway across South Manchuria to the coast, thus making all Manchuria a Russian province. Great Britain got a long lease on Kowloon, a lease on Wei Hai Wei as a naval base for as long as Russia had Port Arthur and Dalny on the Liaotung peninsula, as well as some minor concessions. France got a long lease on Kwang Chao Wan on the southern coast as a naval base, along with minor concessions. In addition all of them secured recognition of a part of China as their exclusive sphere of influence, that is, the area in which they alone would have the privilege of building railways and otherwise exploiting natural resources. Russia got the region north of the Great Wall, Germany the territory adjacent to Shantung, Great Britain the Yangtsze valley, and France the southwestern provinces.

The principle of balance of power was otherwise and more extensively applied. The collection of China's customs duties had for many years been under the supervision of British subjects, first as an emergency measure in the civil war of the 1850's and then continued by mutual consent. China had now formally to concede that its customs should remain under British supervision as long as Great Britain had more trade in China than any other country. In compensation China had to concede to France supervision over the Chinese post office.

Simultaneously the scramble for economic concessions started, especially for railway rights, and finance moved in where guns and diplomacy had prepared the way. Russia having obtained the Manchurian railway concession, the Belgians and French pressed for and obtained the right to build a line between Peking and Hankow. The British, regarding this as a violation of their sphere, first protested and then demanded compensation. Finally, after presenting an ultimatum and bringing up ships, they were authorized to build 2,800 miles of railway, including the line from Tientsin to Nanking and Shanghai. This line had to be shared with Germany after a diplomatic squabble. France and Germany were diligently proceeding with their own railway plans in their respective spheres. While each Power sought to extract as much as possible from China for itself, it sought equally vigorously to prevent every other Power from getting anything at all.

In less than sixty years, then, China's gates had been battered down, forty-two ports had been opened to trade, by cession or lease eight areas had been alienated, and two-thirds of the country had been marked out in spheres of influence of one Power or another. In fourteen of the principal ports concessions and settlements had been staked out for foreign residence. They were in effect foreign cities. Streets and buildings were European in appearance. Administration was entirely in the hands of Europeans, independent of Chinese government authority, and, further, based entirely on the interests of foreigners. Where foreign interests demanded the sacrifice of Chinese, Chinese were sacrificed. Under extraterritoriality foreign residents could conduct themselves as they pleased, even in their relations with Chinese. The Chinese had no recourse. They did not dare send a Chinese policeman into the foreign concession though the boundary were across the street. They could not even pursue a Chinese offender on their own soil who had fled into the concession. And the foreigners in the concessions, though making their money by buying from Chinese and selling to Chinese, paid no taxes to China. But Chinese residing in a foreign concession, as servants, office employes or purveyors of merchandise to the foreigner, did pay taxes to the concession but were given no voice in its government. In result every strategic port of entry in China, almost every important commercial center in China, was a foreign stronghold managed by and for foreigners.

Furthermore, China's tariff on imports was determined not by China but by the foreign Powers. In the treaty of 1842 it had been provided that China was to establish a uniform tariff at all ports. This was later interpreted as meaning that China could not alter its tariff without the consent of the Powers. A tax of five per cent was imposed on all imports and exports, and in 1858 a schedule of prices was adopted as the basis for calculating the tax. It also was provided that this schedule be revised every ten years in accordance with current prices, but there had never been a revision since 1858. China could not make a new schedule without the consent of the Powers, and under the most-favored-nation proviso that meant unanimous consent. For every nation was entitled to all the privileges of every other nation, including that of getting its own products in at the lowest rate. So while most of the Powers could make a show of being willing to revise the schedule, it could always be managed that one be obdurate. In result, therefore, China was getting the revenue not of a five per cent tariff but much less, for prices had been steadily rising, whereas the tariff was calculated on prices of 1858. It may be added here that there was no revision until 1902 and then not again until 1918, despite the war rise in prices.

China seemed tender for the carving and knives were being whetted, when from the Chinese people came one last despairing protest. The Boxer movement, anti-dynastic in the beginning and then anti-foreign, swept North China. Foreigners were attacked, many missionaries and some others were murdered, the European community in Peking was besieged and many Europeans there were killed or died of hardships. It was cruel reprisal and as usual the victims were innocent, but that there should have been reprisals is humanly understandable. It would be more difficult to understand if there had been none.

China's revenge was short-lived. The famous international expeditionary forces, made up of armies from all the great Powers including the United States, arrived in Taku Bay in 1900, took Tientsin, and started overland to Peking to relieve the beleaguered legations. It was an episode out of the Middle Ages. The Boxers being merely a rabble and a poorly armed one, the expeditionary forces had slight opposition. Their progress to the capital was swift and broken only by the time expended in committing atrocities surpassed only in mediæval warfare. They murdered, raped, burned and looted, at random and indiscriminately. For every foreigner killed at least a hundred innocent Chinese peasants were killed and as many of their wives and daughters raped, and a thousand Chinese despoiled of their possessions. And as a climactic demonstration of the white man's chivalry in warfare, the capture of Peking by the foreign detachments was followed by an orgy of looting such as Peking had not known since the northern barbarians had swooped down on it out of mid-Asia. Not drunken privates only but officers, men and women of the diplomatic corps, business men and their wives, missionaries and their wives, rushed through the streets of one of the most beautiful cities in the world, rushed in and out of palaces, temples, official buildings, shops and private residences, shrill, red-faced and tumultuous, their pockets filled with jade and gold and ivories and precious stones. They met in groups in the narrow lanes, compared their spoils and rushed off to other treasure troves, tossing into the streets what they had already gathered in if they found something more valuable. And the Chinese cowered in their homes, hiding their treasures against the sacking that might come at any minute. . . . On the wall of the

British Legation compound there has since been graven the legend, "Lest We Forget." . . . But who?

The next year China had to sign a treaty of reparations to the vindicators of civilization. Besides sundry humiliations like the execution of high officials, expiatory memorials on the thoroughfares of the capital, and diplomatic missions of apology, China was compelled to pay an indemnity of $330,000,000, a sum admittedly far in excess of the damage done by the Boxers. (America subsequently remitted part of its share; Great Britain proposes to do likewise.) Also China had to permit foreign Powers henceforth to maintain garrisons in Peking and along the route between Peking and the sea. It was another famous victory.

The treaty that liquidated the Boxer uprising was noteworthy also for the active entry of the United States into Chinese affairs. The United States to that date had played a negative rôle. Its record was wholly stainless. It sought no territory and no spheres of influence and refused concessions when offered them. But it did permit itself to profit by the aggressions of others. It never took part in bombardments, but as soon as the ports were forced open Americans moved in with the others and demanded the same rights. America had no part in the stealing, but it did accept stolen goods—and has always been smug and unctuous and pharisaical about it. While holding ourselves aloof when dirty work was being done by others and then insisting on getting as much as those who incurred the onus, we have thanked God that we were not as other men and that our government was not as other governments. Was it my country that battered down the gates of Canton? No. But while in Canton did I not enjoy as an American every privilege of any Englishman, Frenchman or Japanese? But in 1900, when it seemed that China was to be partitioned, the United States stepped in and, through Secretary of State John Hay, induced Europe instead to guarantee China's integrity and adopt the policy of the Open Door, the principle of equality of opportunity for all nations in China. The Open Door need not be further defined since it has been honored only in the breach. And it is uncertain whether China escaped partition because of America's efforts or because of European jealousies and inability to come to a division without fighting. But China did escape partition.

Foreign encroachments did not cease, however. They only entered another phase, the more advanced phase of economic penetration—banks, railways, mining companies, investment syndicates, industrial corporations, commercial houses spreading branches over the whole expanse of the country, development of commerce and exploitation of resources, but all drawn into the orbit of the foreigner; and loans, loans, loans, one loan pyramided on another, all carrying with them at least temporary foreign control, and piling up an aggregate overhead that no country in China's stage of economic evolution can carry, and therefore presaging ultimate foreclosure of the mortgage on China's wealth. An outwardly invisible web of conquest was being woven around a country containing one-fourth of the human race, a web of greater tensile strength than any that can be fastened by guns and garrisons.

This was the advanced phase of encroachment, moreover, in that a more intense struggle set in among the aggressors for the exclusive right of dominance. Peking seethed with intriguery, with bribery and counter-bribery, each country backing another Chinese clique in expectation of return in the form of concessions, each country obstructing any economic development which might profit some other country, all orderly development impeded from which China itself might benefit. England against Germany, Germany against Russia, Russia and Germany against England, England and Japan against Russia, the Anglo-Japanese alliance, and in 1904 the harvest, the Russo-Japanese war. For Russia was moving relentlessly into South Manchuria and North China and taking the first steps in Korea, from which it could suspend a sword over Japan. Japan had to fight or succumb. It fought and to the world's amazement won. The victory had implications further reaching than its effect on the status of China, as we shall see, but for the present it suffices to observe that Russia was evicted from the Far East, and Japan took over South Manchuria and a few years later Korea, and became a dominant influence in the Far East and a world Power. But it may be questioned whether all that either Russia or Japan has gained, will gain, or can gain was worth half of what that war alone cost, without taking into the balance the human cost in death and suffering.

Then ten eventful years: China's final renunciation of the past by overthrowing the monarchy and establishing a republic; the world war, and Japan's desperate but unsuccessful attempt to reduce China to vassalage while Europe and the United States were engaged in a struggle for survival. And now the product of those years and the changes wrought not only in China but throughout the world: the resurgence of national consciousness in China, and the demand for emancipation from foreign control, from foreign encroachment on Chinese sovereignty; simultaneously the complete disorganization of government and breakdown in social discipline resulting from an attempt to change the basis of a civilization in a few years and under pressure.

It is just now, when to give up our privileges is most difficult and involves the greatest risk to our interests, that we are asked to give them up. But that is neither accident nor coincidence, it is the logic of the situation. The historic foundations of China had been undermined by a hundred years of Western sapping. The impact of Western ideas and Western forms, of railroads and factories and all the other concomitants of industrialism, and the discrediting of Chinese authority by a hundred years of foreign humiliation and conquest, were disruptive forces against which no society could stand. And the same impulses that prompted the younger generation to revolt against the old order because it could no longer support the Chinese nation in dignity have fired their nationalism and the movement for independence. For subjugation is also of the old order and the white Powers are its agents. It has come to this, out of a hundred years of the relations between the West and China, that every sign of inner health, of inner vitality, in the Chinese race must carry with it anti-foreignism, and anti-foreignism is almost a major symptom of inner health.

Yet between the overthrow of an old order and the establishment of a new one there must always be a long period of insecurity. There is insecurity in China now; and again, a demand for abrogation of all foreign rights and privileges just when our rights and privileges are most necessary for the protection of our vested interests. Be logical? Wait until the transition to the new order has been made and there is security and then ask retrocession? But in the first place, men collectively are never logical, a fact which must be taken as one of the conditions of planetary existence. And in the second place, when the Chinese have asked us, peacefully, humbly, and on the grounds of reason, to relinquish some of our infringements on their sovereignty gradually and progressively, they have been answered with stony silence, scorn or euphemism. The small relinquishments that were asked a few years ago and would have satisfied them were refused. Now they are no longer to be satisfied with little. They ask all, and ask it importunately. Have they not since 1926 arbitrarily deprived us of many of our rights according to treaty, driven us out of the interior, and forced us to send troops for the protection of our citizens and their property? The little they asked a few years ago we stand ready to give now, but that they will not take, for they know we give it only because of the threat against us. They have proved to themselves that they have the power to extract something. Why not insist on all? But for us, to yield all is to incur heavy losses; to refuse all may require an expenditure of force costing more than the value of what is at stake.

But of these the fruits of imperialism we must pluck one. And there, in litttle, is the story of imperialism everywhere.

CHAPTER IV

THE MOTIVES

WHY imperialism? How explain it as an historical force? What are its originating motives? What has driven nations furiously to overrun the earth, subduing what does not bend before them and spending themselves in wars when they collide with each other in the same pursuit? What has driven men to go into distant parts of the world and endure harsh, isolated and often dangerous lives among people they despise and in environments alien and even offensive to them? To answer these questions is not only to illuminate the nature of imperialism but to throw into relief the problems to which it has given rise.

The cause most often cited in the early days was pressure of population. England, Germany, Italy and Japan have a larger population than they can support at home. They must have room to expand. They must have more territory. This explanation can be dismissed summarily. It is too palpably contrary to the facts. Italy has fought a war for Tripoli. Yet fewer Italians choose to make their home in Italian Tripoli than are to be found in lower New

York City. There were 2,000 Germans in German East Africa before the war; at least forty times as many have emigrated to the United States in a single year. Japan is quoted most frequently as the example of a country that must build up an empire to relieve overcrowding. Japan bled itself white to win South Manchuria and Korea. But in South Manchuria after more than twenty years there are fewer than 200,000 Japanese, while in the United States are more than 100,000 despite the exclusion act. Even in Korea there are fewer than 400,000, small enough relief when the population of Japan increases by 600,000 a year. France has recently bombarded and partly destroyed the ancient city of Damascus in order to quiet the Syrians, over whom it has what is euphemistically termed a mandate; and France is notoriously underpopulated. If the reason for expansion be need of outlet for surplus population, why India and equatorial Borneo when there are Canada and Australia? And how on this theory explain the United States in the Philippines or Nicaragua? Most conclusive is the fact that the lands over which there has been the fiercest competition among empires are uninhabitable to white men or, like India and China, already overpopulated. Few white men ever will or can live in inner Africa or southern India or the Malay peninsula or the Philippines. The argument drawn from population needs simply does not bear examination.

THE WHITE MAN'S DILEMMA

Military strategy is another reason for imperialistic ambitions. It has a little more substantial basis. India, for instance, is a British possession. Great Britain therefore cannot permit any other Power to acquire decisive influence in Egypt, it cannot even permit Egypt itself to be wholly independent, else the water route to Egypt through the Suez Canal is cut. So Egypt has been in effect a British protectorate or, as now, nominally independent but with a British garrison posted on the Canal, and a British veto power on Egypt's conduct of foreign relations. Nor can Great Britain view with equanimity a hostile Persian goverment or a Persia too friendly to Russia, lest India be exposed by land. So Great Britain has always maintained something more than a detached interest in Persian internal affairs and has actively intervened whenever Russia became too influential.

If the Philippines are yours you cannot have Japan too strong in Hawaii, lest it be in a position to intercept your navy when the Philippines are menaced. To the contrary, you need Guam for a naval base. Or, if you have an island off the coast of another continent, you cannot have another Power entrenched on the mainland behind you. You cannot even let the sovereign country there get too strong. Suppose Manhattan were a German possession. Could Germany allow England to establish a protectorate or leasehold on the New Jersey shore? Could it let the United States fortify the Jersey shore? Naturally not; in fact, to be on the safe side it would have to take New Jersey itself. In order words, acquiring one outlying territorial possession is only the first of a long series of steps to which a Power is thereby committed. The necessity for those steps becomes "national policy." Strategical considerations, then, are important in motivating imperialistic efforts, but it should be noted that they come into play only after there has been some imperialistic expansion. They are secondary motives.

Secondary also is national honor, or glory or patriotism or however one may wish to designate it. The underfed East End cockney does no doubt experience a glow of pride when told by his *Daily Mail* that the Union Jack flies over Kenya and Borneo and Singapore and Jamaica. Similarly the soda-fountain clerk in an Iowa town is raised in his self-esteem by the thought that Uncle Sam can tell these greasers in Mexico where to get off, and ten U. S. Marines can clean up a whole Central American revolution. Both have a vicarious sense of power which, in the aggregate and skillfully played upon, can be of enormous influence. What else they get out of it except perhaps higher taxes is not quite so clear.

Yet it would never occur to a million cockneys, or clerks, shopkeepers, lawyers or auditors, to exclaim of their own inner prompting, "Come, come, there is Kenya in Africa; why can't a great country like England have it?—let's take it." Nor will millions of

Americans spontaneously generate a passion for Nicaragua as a necessary addition to their country's stature. National honor can be invoked to keep a strong country from getting out of a weak one it has occupied. But it never sends the country there. National honor may be the reason one day for our retaining Vera Cruz and Mexico City; but no outburst of patriotism will ever propel us southward beyond self-control and unconsciously. And even in the former case the conviction of the obligation of national honor will be artificially stimulated by those who have very definite practical reasons for setting stimuli into operation. Patriotism figures in imperialism only after there is already empire.

Another motive is the humanitarian, the desire to spread the benefits of civilization, meaning by civilization the sum of our own ideas and beliefs, our habits and material forms. Here are people unwashed, illiterate, their scalps running sores, swallowing tiger's eyelashes for what they do not recognize to be tuberculosis, torturing witnesses to extract evidence, their streets slimy ruts, their towns sewerless and noisesome, their old men and women harnessed to carts as draft animals, the countryside flooded periodically and depopulated by plagues, their soil rich in treasure they cannot extract even if they know it is there. Why not give them the benefits of our greater knowledge, our efficiency, our command over nature through machinery, our superior social forms? Have we not a moral responsibility to do so? Can we in good conscience leave India to civil wars, China to chaos, Mexico to ignorance and banditry, Central America to its comic opera revolutions, the Philippines to political debauchery?

The white man's burden, in other words. And the complacent assumption underlying all the beliefs and actions of Europeans and Americans, more particularly Anglo-Saxons, that civilization is synonymous with their habits, that there never has been any other civilization, and that no way of life can be civilized unless founded on the same habits. The assumption would be harmless if it did not carry with it the fixed belief that all others must come to the same civilization, and if they do not want to do so they must be made to. The assumption and belief are both difficult to explain. It may be because the Occidental peoples, those unscientifically described as white, are still an upstart race—who so conscious of table manners in others as he who has just learned not to eat with his knife? Or it may be because they feel subconsciously a little uneasy about themselves and their relative position and must bolster up their self-esteem by compelling others to take their pattern. No matter what the reason, the white man is by nature a proselyting animal. And his fanatical obsession of superiority and possession of the only civilization, however absurd it may be philosophically and in the light of history and comparative culture, is nevertheless one of the major forces in our time. Nor has it ever been so fanatical and so arrogantly expressed as now.

This, too, however, is only a secondary motive, though a powerful one. After all, no mass meeting has ever been convened by an American chamber of commerce to report upon the lack of sewers and labor-saving devices in Nicaragua and Haiti, and to call upon the American people to do their duty by their fellowmen and annex Nicaragua and Haiti in order to uplift them. The masses of Americans have not even been aware that there were no sewers and labor-saving devices in Nicaragua, Haiti or any other backward place until their government has been pressed to evacuate territories into which it has gone for reasons having nothing to do with sanitation. Yet more conclusive, there is no record of any strong nation ever having felt called upon to civilize any people whose soil did not hold valuable natural resources.

Like national honor, the humanitarian motive may be invoked in order to remain where a nation has gone as aggressor, but it never prompts any nation to go there. It is a justification after the fact. But it may be invoked more successfully than national honor, because it makes a strong appeal to those who are less moved by acquisitive instincts and more by social consciousness. There are many individuals, often in positions of influence, who are revolted by the cruelties incidental to reducing another people to subjection, but are reconciled by the belief that the end justifies the means, and that the conquered people will be better off ultimately—a belief which must be questioned, because it is necessary to ask what they pay for the benefits they get. Precisely because this appeal has intrinsically so much merit it is potent, and because its merit has little relation to its use it is dangerous. Essentially the humanitarian motive serves as a bid by the interests which profit by aggression for the support of those which do not. We never discover that a backward country ought to be civilized until we have already occupied it by force or are planning to do so.

If these motives are all secondary, then what is the primary motive? At bottom, what it usually is in the affairs of men—economic. The form of conquest which we call imperialism is the product of the industrial revolution. It is no accident that England, the first country to industrialize, was the first empire and the greatest, and that the period of the most aggressive imperialistic expansion was also the period in which industrialism was attaining its highest development. There is a direct relation of cause and effect.

Trade between widely separated regions is hardly a phenomenon of recent times. Europe and Asia were exchanging commodities before the age of Christ. But until recent times such trade was almost entirely in luxuries and partook of the nature of adventure. The productive economy of every region was organized on the basis of the visible demand in its own area. Means of transportation were too limited for exportation on a large scale, even if means of production had not been too rudimentary to yield much surplus over needs. And what was there to trade in except gems and silks and spices, frankincense and myrrh? When there was little subdivision of labor and less specialization, what was there produced in one region that another could not produce, excepting luxuries?

Then came the machine, in application of the scientific discoveries which were to harness nature to man's driving. And the principal result of machinery is large-scale production. With enough machinery and the capital to operate it, there is no limit to the quantity you can produce if you have the raw materials, labor and the market. Now, some materials were available everywhere, and labor was plentiful and cheap, but after the domestic demand was satisfied there was every incentive to reach out for foreign markets. The inventions which made factories possible also gave quicker and easier means of transportation, so that access to markets was easier than it had been. And outside Western Europe and the United States was a virgin field for exploitation—in Asia alone more than half the human race to sell goods to.

THE MOTIVES

Markets meant profits, and the more exclusive the command over the market the larger the profits. The only way to make sure of your market was to control it, and the only way to control it was to have authority over those who composed it. For simultaneously nationalism had taken root, with the attendant concept that the state was the instrument of nationality, which in the era of the ascendancy of the bourgeoisie was interpreted as the duty of the government to advance business. The now sacrosanct law that a government must protect the business interests of its citizens abroad, no matter what those interests may be or how obtained, is not eternal, immutable and handed down by God. It is of comparatively recent origin and was evolved by very decidedly mundane financial groups trying to acquire or consolidate interests abroad which they could not acquire or consolidate without armies and navies. Competition for markets having formed on national lines, tariffs were fabricated as weapons of offense and defense. And a tariff barrier could not be laid across a foreign country for your own commercial advantage unless you had hegemony over it. To hold a foreign market, then, and extract the greatest advantage, you were impelled to obtain political and military power over the area in which it lay. The way to make it your market was to make it your territory.

Domestic consumption increased as the standard of

living was raised. Foreign trade increased as penetration into the outlying regions went further and deeper. Productive capacity increased as machinery multiplied and improved in technical efficiency. But raw materials could not be replaced as could men and machines. When exhausted, new supplies had to be tapped. And Asia, Africa, the Pacific islands and Latin America were untouched storehouses of raw materials, many of them indispensable and invaluable. As industry became more complex and demanded a larger quantity and wider variety of raw materials—the iron, copper, oil, rubber and the like which are the lifeblood of modern industry—an incentive was furnished for obtaining access to the known deposits of such materials. For the same reasons that operated in foreign trade it was deemed imperative to have exclusive access, which again meant political and military authority over the lands where there were such deposits. The way to make the oil or gold or copra or tin yours was to make the territory yours.

Industrialism, besides creating a demand for markets and raw materials, had one other conspicuous effect. It made possible the accumulation of vast quantities of fluid capital. At first this capital was needed at home. Railroads were to be built, public utilities organized, resources exploited, and large industrial plants erected and equipped with costly machinery. Profits were huge, kingly fortunes were built up. The more thorough the process of industrialization the larger the store of liquid capital. But with intensive development the law of diminishing returns set in, and money could no longer be invested at home except at regularized market rates. There was a surplus of capital. The surplus sought an outlet.

Obviously the most advantageous outlet was in lands not yet industrially developed and altogether unexploited. Why invest money in Manchester cotton mills or American railroads at four or five or eight per cent when Congo rubber, say, yielded fifteen or twenty? Thus, moreover, a double purpose was served. A handsome return was netted and rubber or copper or iron was obtained for factories at home, thus enhancing the value of industries at home. Or, if not Congo rubber, then railways in China, which served the additional purpose of carrying into the interior more of the goods manufactured at home, thus increasing the profits on money invested at home. Or, if not rubber plantations and railways, then establishing factories in China or India, where raw materials were close at hand, labor was paradisically cheap, an elysian freedom from government restriction could be enjoyed, and there were no prying humanitarian liberals, reformers, idealists and utopians to insist that the working classes were not happiest when kept working fourteen hours a day.

Is it not significant that the United States was entirely inward-centered while it was still industrially undeveloped, before natural resources were appropriated and great corporations organized? It took no part in the world race for territory and even refused concessions in China. Only at the end of the nineteenth century did it reach out beyond its own borders and its public men begin to talk about manifest destiny. And can one say only coincidence of the fact that just then the most glittering financial opportunities in America were beginning to pass? And is it coincidence also that America should have become vitally concerned, even directly involved, in Far Eastern politics and be unmistakably stretching out over Latin America since the world war gave it a monopoly of surplus capital and credit?

Now, investments abroad may be merely financial operations. The first American railroads were built with a large proportion of foreign money. But the English holders of Illinois Central bonds received their interest, that was all. The terms were fixed by the Americans who built the railway, administration was entirely in their hands, policy was determined by them exclusively. In return for the use of their money foreigners got interest. Or, if they were shareholders, they had a proportionate voice in directors' or shareholders' meetings. If occasion arose they always had recourse to American courts. But that was sufficient. In America there was an established government resting on principles basically common to the Western world. Economic principle and practice differed little from that of Europe. The premises underlying social relations in Europe and America were alike or closely related. Also there was in America a marked disposition, a determination even, to manage its own affairs. And an army and navy were not lacking to give the determination some foundation.

In backward countries, however, investments are more than financial operations. Probably they must be. At any rate they are. Could money be invested in the Congo, in Tunis, in Borneo, in China, in Persia, as it was in the United States? Government was of persons, not laws, expressing itself in caprice and recognizing no responsibility or accountability. The traditions of government put no stigma on corruption—that is, the standards of political practice were different from ours. In business there was no tradition of corporate trusteeship and responsibility. Of course, investments in such regions were insecure without, as it were, extraterritorial privileges, that is, a status of immunity from native interference. Only such enterprises as were completely autonomous could survive. And inasmuch as nearly all enterprises in which foreigners were interested were started on foreign initiative, they were autonomous from the beginning. What was to restrain or prohibit them? Siam had no army and navy like the

American army and navy. China attempted restraint and failed. Even when an enterprise was nominally under native ownership, like Chinese railroads, if there was foreign capital—as there had to be, for economically undeveloped countries lack the fluid capital for projects involving a large original outlay—there had to be foreign supervision. And if the enterprises were quasi-public in nature, like railroads, or by their nature automatically stretched out tentacles of power and influence, like mines and steamship lines, supervision and autonomy implied at least a semblance of political control. And if conditions were not such as to demand quasi-control, if, that is, there was not "chaos," providence might intervene so that there would be chaos. Revolutions in backward regions are not always of spontaneous combustion. The elements may often be introduced and combined from without. Indeed, insecurity of foreign investments often has its uses. By creating a necessity for one's government to protect one's life and property it may also create opportunities for acquiring more property, which in the future will again be jeopardized, which will again create a necessity for one's government to protect one's life and property, and so on.

The economic motive in imperialism is clear. It was a motive that operated not only in the sense that there was gain in imperialistic adventures, but also in the sense that imperialistic conquest may have been essential to the establishment of the social system which differentiates Europe and America in modern times—and may be essential to the maintenance of the system now. That question must be considered at this point.

CHAPTER V

BACKWARDNESS AND RICHES

THE civilization of the modern West rests on the industrial system. Our lives in their every aspect, intellectual and spiritual no less than physical, are influenced, even moulded, by the fact of machine production and all that flows from it. That the industrial system cannot function without raw materials is a point that need not be labored. Without coal, oil, iron, copper, tin, platinum, antimony, manganese, rubber, copra, cotton, silk, nitrates, indigo, potash, plant derivatives and the innumerable other materials that enter into its intricate processes, modern industry could not exist. Many of these basic materials are to be found only in countries which have come under the domination of the great Powers, and all of them are to be found in large quantities in such countries. Unless they had been made available to our use, the evolution of the industrial system would have been markedly retarded; and unless they were available to our use now, the whole form and structure of our society would be altered. It may be asked whether it would not have been better, even for ourselves, had the industrial system evolved more slowly, and whether a fundamental change in our present society would be an unmixed tragedy. But that is not at issue at this point; it will be touched on later.

The question then emerges: Given that our economic system is dependent upon access to natural resources everywhere, and that these resources are to be found in lands inhabited by peoples in an earlier stage of development, can we obtain the resources without taking over the lands in which they are to be found; and if not, then have such peoples any inherent right to lock up their riches from the world out of any concepts of self-determination, national integrity, independence and the like, concepts originally ours, not theirs? That is to say, is America to be impeded in its progress toward the goal it has set for itself, and its population made less comfortable, because Mexicans are too inefficient to bring their oil to the surface themselves, and Persians are too ignorant to know even that there is oil under the surface? Or Japan: in order to survive, Japan has had to set foot on the road to industrialization. In order to advance it must have coal, iron, oil. Thirty-six hours away is China, with vast stores of coal, iron and probably oil. The Chinese could not or would not mine their coal and iron so that it could be bought in the commercial market. Shall Japan, then, renounce its ambition, fall back in the world race, and surrender itself to obscurity out of regard for China's right to remain behind the times?

THE WHITE MAN'S DILEMMA

Two questions are involved, one practical and the other ethical. First, what follows from the attempt to "take" countries if their riches are indispensable? Second, is the necessity of survival moral justification for taking what we need from those who cannot make proper use of that which is theirs, or must we impose sacrifices on ourselves out of respect for the "rights" of those unable to defend themselves? The second question can be dealt with briefly. It can be dismissed. In the first place, it involves too many metaphysical subtleties. The oil of Mesopotamia may be called the heritage of the Mesopotamian. Is it not despoiling him to deprive him of it? Or *is* the oil of Mosul the Mesopotamian's heritage by virtue of the fact that it flows under the land on which he dwells? Is it his more than the Englishman's? Does geology take cognizance of national boundaries? Are not the riches of nature all man's, and can one tribe or nation or race deprive all mankind of those riches by the accident of residence? If so, then the logical conclusion may be that no race of men can ever progress faster than the least progressive. But it should be remembered that the principle of ownership inhering in the national occupant is imbedded deep in such international law as there is and deeper still in practice, and if the principle works one way it must work the other. But this is beside the point. The fact is that we do take Mesopotamia's oil and South Africa's gold and Malay rubber and Sumatran rubber, and we shall continue to do so however unshakably it may be demonstrated to be morally wrong.

The practical question is more to the point. Could we have obtained the raw materials without imperialistic domination, without control wholly or in part, in fact if not in legal sovereignty? Manifestly not. Could the native of Borneo have cultivated rubber plantations, or the tribesman of the Congo mine copper? Would they have wanted to? Why? Their needs were simple and were satisfied by nature's beneficence. Food grew almost of itself, shelter could be made in a day. What more did they want? The complicated demands that impel men to wrest riches from the soil by hard labor must be instilled into a primitive people from without. In other words, a primitive people must be "developed" before it has any desire to develop. Until it first has railroads, electric lights and telephones it will not want railroads, electric lights and telephones—and porcelain bathtubs, perfumes, tooth-pastes, sewing-machines, safety razors, automobiles and chewing-gum. By giving them railroads and rubber plantations and copper mines we have also made it necessary for them to take from us the multitude of products which we alone can manufacture. Thus we profit at both ends.

On a level above the primitive, consider Mexico. It is a country of peasants, with a small urban merchant and official class and a still smaller intelligentsia. Whence were the Mexicans to derive the knowledge to pump oil out of wells hundreds of feet deep under the soil and run pipe lines to the Rio Grande or the sea coast? Had it been left to their initiative the oil probably would still be hundreds of feet under the soil. The same is true even of highly civilized countries whose civilization is not founded on mechanization. Consider China. The Chinese, too, are predominantly a peasant people. Their towns are more numerous and larger, but the town population consists of merchants and artisans and craftsmen (and poets and painters and scholars and philosophers, but that is another matter) working with skill, ingenuity and an intuitive feeling for beauty that have given the world some of its most exquisite objects; but the production unit is the household, the scale of production is small, and tools are simple and manipulated by man-power. Men who cultivate their fields with implements such as their ancestors used two thousand years ago, who live in isolated villages, communicating only with those in their immediate radius and using as their means of transport mule-back, the springless cart and the wheelbarrow, who still, when they see their first automobile in Shanghai or Tientsin, press their faces against the radiator to find the evil spirit that makes it go—obviously such men cannot bring the iron ore out of the earth and smelt it, no matter how much English and American factories cry for steel.

They must be able not only to sink and operate a mine. They must know how to erect and operate smelters, railroads, telegraph and telephone systems, electric power plants, machine shops and centralized exchanges. They must have mechanical and organizing efficiency and a technology that cannot be acquired in five years or ten or thirty. Even Japan, which has to its credit a truly miraculous transformation from the Middle Ages to the twentieth century, needed a generation before it could begin to compete with the industrial West on terms of equality. It apprenticed the best of its younger generation all over the world, brought in large numbers of foreigners as experts and teachers, went through years of expensive tutelage. And despite the advantages of eagerness, singleness of purpose, clearness of aim, and the leadership of an extraordinary group of men called out by a crucial time, Japan is still but halfway industrialized and economically badly balanced. The eighteenth century is even now not many hours' riding from Osaka, a city one with Chicago and Manchester.

And during the thirty or forty or fifty years in which the Chinese—or Turks or Arabs or Persians or Javanese or Malays—were mastering the technology which would equip them to release their resources for sale in the open market in a purely commercial transaction, as one buys German dyes or American copper, what then? Would we have waited

THE WHITE MAN'S DILEMMA

for them to do so? Would we wait now? Would we have the patience, and the resignation to the heavy financial loss entailed? You need only visualize a directors' meeting of the Royal Dutch-Shell or Standard Oil Company. The chairman of the board speaks. "Yes, gentlemen, our geologists' reports are confirmed. There is oil in Mosul, enough for the world's needs for years. But you must understand that Irak (Mesopotamia, old style) is still decidedly primitive, and although the natives are awakening to their opportunities and hear the call of prosperity, we cannot anticipate that they will know how to get their oil to us for many, many years. It is a pity, but I see nothing else to be done." And the board after deliberation decides regretfully that we must wait, but votes a resolution of encouragement to the government and people of Irak, with an offer of cordial coöperation. A resolution in which it is promptly joined by all the other international oil syndicates. You need only visualize that.

Of the two ways open to us if we wanted the resources—to wait a generation or two or else to take the resources by force—it goes without saying that we followed the latter. Given the competitive system and the premise that private business interests need never suffer any obstruction they are strong enough to overcome, that course was inevitable. Not inevitable in the sense of following physical or astronomical law and being beyond human control, but in the sense that acquisitive instincts move us more than any other and that we live in an anarchic society. For with any agency or capacity for social planning, it might have been judged more profitable to wait the generation or two; more profitable, that is, to us as a whole and not to the special interests involved. In the end perhaps we should have paid less. We might have avoided the cost of wars and armaments to prepare for wars, and had access to the resources by less tortuous paths. With native good will rather than hostility, and with international coöperation rather than poisonous diplomatic intriguery and dog-in-the-manger obstructionism, we might have been able to obtain raw materials in greater quantity and cheaper. And we might have avoided the ugly pass in which we now find ourselves. But this is to talk of a world that did not exist, and does not now.

Where there was a primitive society, as in the African interior, access to resources was relatively simple. A native chief was induced to sign a paper he could not read, accepting the "protection" of a distant state he had never heard of. Even that formality could be dispensed with sometimes, since it was resorted to only in order to gain a color of legality against a rival Power desiring the same protectorate. If so, we just landed troops and called the territory ours. Then we staked out our plantations or mines and put the natives to work. Either we rounded them up and flogged them if they refused to work;

or we levied a tax by virtue of our status as protector, a tax which would be paid only in labor, for the native had no property; or we made a deal with the native chief whereby he got arms or rum or trinkets or gold or some of each, especially rum, in return for delivering a certain number of his tribesmen to work so many months a year. Essentially it was forced labor. There was no alternative if we had to have labor, since white men could not work in such climes, and anyway white men's labor came high. How persuade a native to work of his own free will? He had everything he needed. His desires were simple. He asked of life only to eat, sleep, hunt, fish and occasionally kill his fellow-man with spear or bow and arrow for no particular reason except momentary dislike. Why should he voluntarily exchange that lot for one of hard toil and killing his fellow-man with rifles for reasons having something remotely to do with treaties, concessions, spheres and "national destinies"?

Where there was not a primitive society but an established order rooted in an old culture and highly organized, it was not so simple to go in and get the resources. Protectorates could not be set up by fiat. Some measure of respect had to be paid to governments, even if their armies were effective only as exhibition, as we saw illustrated by the story of China. It was not a matter of introducing a system of production and distribution where there had been vacuum before. A new one had to be superimposed on an old. Thus two conflicts were raised: one against the resistance of the old, and the other among those who wanted the privilege and profit of introducing the new—in other words, the struggle for concessions.

It must be understood that for an older, unmechanized society to make its resources available to the industrial West, something more was necessary than the mastery of a technology. The society had also to be willing. China and India and Persia and Egypt and Turkey had to be willing to abandon their own civilizations, change their way of life for one wholly alien, and renounce all that had come down to them from their forefathers, all the body of tradition from which a race derives its self-respect. Nothing less than that was involved. Technology cannot be applied in the abstract. It will manifest itself in the concrete forms of steel mills, railways, machine shops, factories, standardized foods, standardized clothes, standardized household appliances, standardized amusements. Then, as has been the case with New England and New Jersey villages now Lawrences and Passaics, and Pennsylvania villages now Pittsburghs, so must it be with Benares and Lahore, Bagdad and Teheran, Kyoto and Hangchow. This is not speculation. Proof is already to be seen in modern Japan, and everywhere in the port cities of the East where foreigners have entrenched themselves.

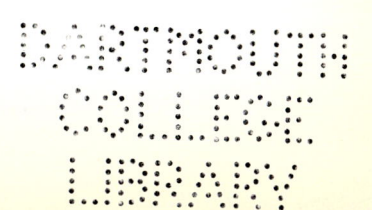

THE WHITE MAN'S DILEMMA

It could not be otherwise. The tranquil, slow-paced life of small self-sustaining communities, working long but leisurely, enjoying the quiet hours in temple courtyard or village teahouses, having scant comforts but fewer strains, cannot co-exist with Chicago. A people cannot live beside a railway and work in factories and preserve mind and spirit unaltered. They cannot use telephones and telegraphs and not acquire habits that change their outlook. Men do not make their institutions conform to a previously conceived philosophy. Their philosophy is formed by their institutions. The price of exploiting resources is industrialism and its inseparable accompaniments. It is a new scheme of life, the one we know in America.

Now the passing of the old scheme of life and the culture on which it rested may have been inevitable, with or without external pressure. It may be that the advance of knowledge by the discoveries of science was not to be denied by national boundaries. And in the end the older races may have benefited by the change, for to the accompaniments of industrialism there are patent advantages. But such a change must come imperceptibly and take its impetus from within unless it is to come with a wrench. Imposed from without and lacking the element of choice, it can only be resented, and where possible it will be sabotaged. To a great degree it still is being both resented and sabotaged, partly unconsciously in the form of inertia and inefficiency, partly consciously, as in the Gandhi movement in India.

Although less formidable as an obstacle to the tapping of supplies of raw materials than lack of technical ability, unwillingness was serious enough in that it fortified inertia. If we could not wait until the unindustrialized people learned how to exploit their resources, still less could we begin one step further back and convert them to the belief that they ought to learn. So we let them walk their ancestral ways, but obtained permission or wrested the right to lay out new paths among them but not yet of them. We let them have their Oriental tranquillity, but we laid railroads, dug mines, and erected the necessary complementary plants. And as the ramifications of those enterprises spread, as we have seen they must, and other plants and banks and shops and housing for laborers gathered around the nucleus, a new little society was created within the older one. It was a society that the governing and ruling classes of the older one were incompetent to supervise or control, since it was alien to them. Nor would we have been willing to allow them to attempt to. For one thing, they really were incompetent, they did not understand its aim or structure. For another, our freedom would have been restricted and therefore our profits. We could do only what we did: set up an *imperium in imperio*, and expand our concessions, originally limited to specific enterprises, to include first autonomy from native interference and then independence. What began as a concession ended as a colony, whether legally so recognized or not. It had to end so. If we do not take these measures in the beginning, circumstances soon intervene to constrain us.

Countries that are called backward are militarily weak and politically not very stable; at least, political foundations are loosely laid. That is why they are called backward. Their governments are hardly made more stable by the disruptive forces of foreign intrusion. In the usual course of events in such countries there is a change of government, which does not take place by some orderly and prescribed procedure, but by haphazard methods odious to us but perhaps more suited to the people themselves—say revolution. There supervenes what we call chaos. A loose word, this chaos. It generally designates a state of affairs different from what we are accustomed to at home and uncomfortable to us. What every American fears if the Philippines are granted their independence is corruption; and what Pennsylvania editorial writer would not wax minatory and moral at the exposure that a seat in the Philippines Senate has been bought by huge political donations? At any rate, there is chaos. Now, as we have already seen, what follows when there is chaos in militarily weak countries where we have investments? <u>Our investments are jeopardized.</u> They really are. We must protect our investments—our lives and our property. And since chaos is in the nature of things in such countries, sooner or later we exercise a permanent supervision over the countries.

The second conflict arising from the necessity of superimposing a new order on an old led more directly to imperialistic control. I have been saying, thus far, "we" had to go and take the resources, "we" built the railroads, "we" got the concessions. But that "we" is an abstraction. In reality there was no single entity that could be so designated. There were several. There were the British, French, German, Russian, Belgian, Dutch, Italian, and later the American. Which "we" would do all these things— get concessions, build railroads, extract iron or oil or diamonds or copper, and introduce a new civilization? Though it be proved unconfutably that the resources of the whole world must be unlocked for the whole world, the question still remains, who is to unlock them? And are they unlocked for the whole world, or for Britons or Germans or Americans? And for whom among those—all Britons or the British oil companies, all Americans or the American banking groups?

We have already seen in Chapter II how the process of modernizing a backward country operates. We have seen it begin with cultivation of the good will of a native ruler or his cabinet; then a loan in return for a concession to exploit a mine; a railway and harbor and banks and a foreign community so that the mine's products may be brought to market; and then economic suzerainty over the territory in which the mine lies. But within twenty minutes after, say, the British representative has made his first tender for the good will of the native ruler, the French representative is apprized thereof. In the realm of such affairs news travels fast, even in capitals without newspapers. The French representative makes a corresponding tender for the good will of the native ruler; in fact he makes a more substantial one. And the native ruler, who soon becomes worldly wise, remains undecided about which tender to accept until both have been made more substantial. Very well, say the British offer is accepted, the Britons get the concession. The French representative returns. Now he talks more bluntly. He intimates that the bonds of friendship that have united their respective countries are strained. It would be a pity if they were severed. But there will be no preventing such a rupture unless French interests are now given a concession for a mine or a railway elsewhere. The French representative is supported by official messages of similar purport from home and perhaps the movement of gunboats in near-by waters. In short, the French representative gets the concession. And then the German, and the Russian. Each has his concession, each tries to get more, each tries continually to squeeze out the others.

BACKWARDNESS AND RICHES

There can be no stability to such a state of affairs. There can be no security to one's position in such a situation until it has been regularized, until assurances have been given that one's concessions will not be alienated to another country. One gets recognition of one's sphere. One gets a guaranty of its inviolability even by the government of the theoretically sovereign state in which the sphere is situated. In other words, that state ceases to be sovereign. Sovereignty, for all practical purposes, will inhere at first jointly in the foreign Powers which have obtained spheres or material concessions, and ultimately in the Power among them which proves strongest. The test of strength may be made in diplomatic and financial intriguery. If that is not decisive there is recourse to war.

In sum, there was no escape from imperialism unless the Western Powers were willing to forego the raw materials to be found in the weak and economically undeveloped regions. There is not now. We must maintain our position in our dependencies or we cannot continue to obtain cheaply, quickly and efficiently, if at all, the basic materials without which our whole economic system would be disorganized. What was true one hundred years ago is less true now only by degree. For most of Africa and Asia have been industrialized only on the fringes. It is not yet possible to deal with them commercially in the normal way of foreign trade. If by some miracle they should suddenly regain mastery of their own destinies, the flow of raw materials to us and of manufactured products to them would be disrupted for long, and for a time cease. It will be necessary later to analyze just what would have been lost had we been forced to forego those raw materials, and who would have lost it; and what would be lost now if the flow of them were disrupted, and who would lose. Even within one country the word "we" is too broad, and an analysis of the pronoun into its constituent elements is essential to an understanding of world politics. But if we face the same choice now as we did one hundred years ago, it is with this vital difference, that it will be much more difficult to maintain our position in our dependencies than it was to establish it.

CHAPTER VI

THE RESULTS—A WORLD OVERRUN

SUCH the motives, so they worked, and these the results: at the end of a hundred years two continents and more than two-thirds of the population of the earth become appendages to a few aggressive nationalities of the West. By 1914, in all Asia and Africa one nation alone could call itself independent, Japan. By an exaggerated euphemism a few others might be classified as independent—Turkey and Persia, say, in Asia, and Abyssinia and Liberia in Africa; but only by euphemism. They were independent in so far as they were free to take any action not disagreeable or unprofitable to some European Power. For the rest, Asia and Africa were parceled out. The white man's burden had been assumed to the uttermost ounce. Only 50,000,000 of all the non-white peoples of the earth had escaped the fate of being uplifted.

First as to Asia. England's absorption of India had begun before the age of imperialism, through the penetration of the British East India Company, a private company chartered to exploit the East. France, which contested England's supremacy in

India, was ousted in the war of 1763-68, and from then until the middle of the nineteenth century England was spreading its hegemony over the country by so-called treaties with native princes or by outright attack and seizure. The British had long since begun to exercise supervision over the East India Company, the callousness of the Company's acts and the corruption among its officials in India having scandalized decent opinion in England, a fact now conveniently forgotten by Englishmen—and Americans—when talking of dishonesty in the government of countries not white. After the Indian Mutiny was put down in 1857, and men blown from the mouths of British cannon by way of punishment and deterrent, the authority of the Company was cancelled altogether and the rule of India vested in the British Cabinet. Finally in 1877 Disraeli, himself an Oriental, with a truly Byzantine flourish made a present of India to his Queen, and thus established himself more securely in that lady's uncertain graces. India became a part of the British Empire.

With China, the other great prize of the East, it has been as we have seen. Central Asia—Turkestan, Bokhara, Khiva—the glamorous terrain north of India and west of China, fell to Russia; just taken, more or less, in the stride across Asia to the Pacific. The semi-barbarous tribes could offer little resistance to the Russian expeditions which pushed out from Russia's Asiatic frontiers during the nineteenth century. Europe could offer little more, though Britain anxiously watched the Bear's shadow lengthen over India. And there and then began the Anglo-Russian feud, artificially suspended in 1914-18 and now blazing again in Soviet Russia's attempt to capitalize Chinese resentment against the British. It is a feud laid in one dispute, which of them shall have mastery over Asia.

The story of Siam, with British India on one side and French Indo-China on the other, is the story of China in miniature, with commensurate results. What was left, after tens of thousands of square miles had been shorn away by France on the one side and by Britain on the other in treaties concluded after the manner of the Chinese treaties, was independent, subject only to the modification of spheres, concessions, and the appointment to various government departments of British and French advisers whose advice, it is true, was disinterested and often beneficial, except where the interests of their respective countries were involved.

The long Malay peninsula, depending from Siam at the south-eastern corner of the continent, is British. Part of it is administered directly by the British government as the Straits Settlements, in which lies the port of Singapore; part as a federated protectorate, the Federated Malay States; and part by native sultans with the advice and assistance of British Residents, advice and assistance which it would never occur to them to refuse. All of it is in effect as British as India, and the process of becoming British was according to pattern: concessions, exploitation of concessions, and political consolidation to protect concessions; treaties of protection which could be refused only under penalty of worse than what great Powers mean by protection; and military occupation, followed by "pacification" if resisted. The reasons for British acquisition were two: first, rubber; second, tin.

South of the continent of Asia is the empire of the Netherlands, the Dutch East Indies: Java, Sumatra, Celebes, and all of Borneo that is not British. These rank as islands, but as their area is 740,000 square miles and their population 50,000,000, and as their products include half of the rubber grown in the world, a large part of the coffee and tobacco, sugar, oil and quinine, they constitute an empire. The Dutch East Indies were acquired in the halcyon period of Dutch explorations in the seventeenth century. Their status was in flux during the Napoleonic wars, but by agreement between England and the Netherlands the Dutch were confirmed in their possession of the islands in the Treaty of Vienna, an indiscretion unique in British diplomacy and subsequently much criticized by numerous British patriots overseas, but forgivable in view of the contemporary ignorance of the importance of rubber and oil.

Off the Asiatic continent also are the Philippine

Islands, but as their status falls under the double classification of idealism and imperialism, they will be discussed later.

At the other extreme of the continent Turkey was nominally a sovereign empire, but parts of its outlying territory were administered by Europeans, its finances were under the supervision of Europeans, its hinterland was a battleground of European concessionaires, and foreigners enjoyed extraterritorial rights under the Capitulations. It was openly referred to as the Sick Man of Europe, and the vultures were slowly wheeling in the air above. Persia, too, was nominally independent, but marked out in spheres and the football of Anglo-Russian politics. The episode of the appointment of W. Morgan Shuster, an American brought in by the Persian government to rehabilitate its finances and then dismissed on the insistence of the British and Russian governments because he was succeeding so well that their perquisites might be jeopardized, is illustrative. A backward people, it should be observed, must submit to derogations of its sovereignty, if not "trusteeship," until it is "reconstructed," has "set its house in order," and learned to "stand on its own feet." But let it just try to stand on its own feet! Persia tried.

The world war produced few changes in Asia. Turkey was shorn of its possessions and reduced practically to the territory inhabited by the Ottoman

Turks. Turkey proper, left crushed by the war, arose in desperation in 1922, drove out the Allied invaders, and for the moment is truly free. Arabia was divided up between Great Britain and France. The division was in the usual proportions. It is all British except Syria. True, the allocations were made under the designation of mandates, a distinction which may have meaning in a dim future. To have a mandate over a territory is to govern it as you would an old-fashioned protectorate, except that once a year you make a report to a committee on which you sit very prominently and which permits itself only rhetorical indiscretions, if any. Otherwise the continent of Asia is still a European appendage.

As to Africa. In the days antedating the higher duty to transmit civilization, Africa was left to its tom-toms, witch doctors, dances, and other simpler if bloody pleasures of savagery. Turkey was entrenched on the north coast, but Europe was indifferent to the dark continent. Great Britain had a foothold on the Cape, and a few small and shadowy claims. France, Spain and Portugal similarly had small and shadowy claims. But they were largely paper claims. The next fifty years witnessed few changes. Great Britain pushed the Boers northward from the Cape and extended its holdings there, and France conquered Algeria on the north coast after a dispute compounded of Algerian piracy, an unpaid

THE RESULTS—A WORLD OVERRUN

French debt to Algeria, and the slapping of a French commissioner's face by the Dey of Algeria.

In 1880 the African rush began, speeded no doubt by the glorious triumphs then being achieved in Asia. How impetuous the rush was may be gathered from the fact that in ten years 6,000,000 square miles of African territory, more than half the continent, had been appropriated by seven Powers—Great Britain, France, Germany, Belgium, Italy, Portugal and Spain. By 1914 the remaining 5,500,000 square miles had been appropriated, with two doubtful exceptions to be noted later. France had 4,200,000 square miles, Great Britain 3,500,000, Germany 1,000,000, Italy 1,000,000, Belgium 800,000, Portugal 800,000 and Spain 75,000. These figures must be interpreted with the knowledge that Great Britain's share, though less in area than France's, included South Africa, with its gold and diamond fields, Egypt, and the Sudan. The lion's share was Britain's, a phenomenon we may have seen recur with some regularity.

There is no need for an exhaustive treatment of the methods of appropriation. As already indicated, except on the Mediterranean shores, where there was a sense of national identity and a cultural heritage, it was a simple matter of grab. Black savages armed with spears and poisoned arrows or even with a few rifles were helpless, and the only restraints suffered were those laid by the ambitions of another Power to grab the same piece of territory. Sometimes when the natives did not appreciate their helplessness, it became unfortunately necessary to kill them in great numbers, but such unpreventable exigencies in the enterprise of bearing light unto darkness were happily not frequent. Fewer casualties were inflicted on the blacks by our guns than by rum, venereal disease, and forced labor under conditions of cruelty. Who knows how many hundreds of thousands or millions so perished, not dramatically but in slow decay? They died that their fellow-blacks might live the higher life of civilization.

Let us say a European Power had one of these shadowy claims already mentioned. The claim had to be given more clear definition, or, as it is technically put, there had to be a rectification of frontiers. How? One moved out ten, twenty, fifty, a hundred, three hundred miles in every direction, and thus frontiers were rectified and a colony was established. Or it might be necessary to make geographical explorations of unmapped territory. Scientific expeditions were dispatched, bearing with them the flags of their country and accompanied by military escorts for protection. The flags were planted along the explorers' route and thus also a colony was acquired.

More often a small band of adventurers with or without commissions from their governments landed on the coast and proceeded inland, procuring from tribal chieftains or more pretentious native rulers signatures to previously drafted treaties ceding thousands of square miles of territory. With the treaties in their portfolios they returned home, secured charters from their governments for the exploitation of the ceded territory and financial backing for the first outlay in exploitation—more likely government recognition depended on how influential was the financial backing—and a few hundred thousand or it might be a few million Africans suddenly found themselves the private property of a corporation formed to do business and make a profit. Business being business, it was often necessary to evict the natives or put them to work or both. But the natives, being savages, were lamentably lacking in business principles, a consideration which prompted Mr. Joseph Chamberlain, the unforgettable English statesman, to say, "It is our [Britain's] duty to take our share in the work of civilization in Africa." The first principles of civilization, that is, business principles, had therefore to be inculcated. The pedagogic method has already been touched on.

In the Belgian Congo of fragrant memory, private property of the sainted King Leopold II, labor was conscripted, each district assessed so much rubber or ivory, and other districts were compelled to grow food for those engaged in rubber or ivory. Native armies also were conscripted to see that the native workers did not shirk their duty. The natives were paid for their labor, but a premium was put on paying them as little as possible, since the less they got the more the Belgian overseers got. And the natives' power of bargaining in wages may be gathered from the fact that if one of them refused to work his family was imprisoned, and if many refused at once they were beaten, mutilated or shot down. How many thousands were tortured, how many thousands mutilated, how many thousands killed will never be known, but a succession of revelations by neutral investigators so shocked Europe that international protests were made, and Leopold agreed upon reforms and turned over his holdings to his government for a consideration of some $20,000,000; a reasonable figure, inasmuch as his annual profits had been estimated at that much.

In Portuguese Africa there was unconcealed slavery. In the French Congo also natives were given quotas and punished on failure to deliver, punishment being by way of flogging or execution. In German Southwest Africa the natives were evicted from their lands by way of inculcating industriousness, and when they rebelled were disciplined by wholesale slaughter. In British Africa, naturally, it was different. Practices were consonant with the lofty principles laid down by Mr. Chamberlain. There was no forced labor, so there was a scarcity of labor and wages were high. What to do?

"If they could make these people work, they

would reduce the rate of labor in the country," said Cecil Rhodes, whose monument is British South Africa. "It is wrong that there should be a million natives in that country [South Africa] and yet that they [British mineowners] should be paying a sum equal to £1 a week for their labor while that labor was essential for the development of the country."

More to the point was a British representative in the Transvaal: "We should try some cogent form of inducement, or practically compel the native, through taxation or in some other way, to contribute his quota to the good of the community, and to a certain extent he should then have to work."

More definite—one would say constructive if he were an American—was Earl Grey, director of the Chartered Company of Rhodesia: "Means have to be found to induce the native to seek spontaneously employment at the mines, and to work willingly for long terms of more or less continuous employment. An incentive to labor must be provided, and it can only be provided by the imposition of taxation."

Observe the difference in tone and spirit from that which animated the French and Belgians: "The proper development of the country"—"the good of the community"—and to that end an inducement to working "spontaneously" in the form of a tax which could be paid by working only. So there was a tax; and thus subjective uplift was combined with social betterment, and in return for his tutelage the British pioneer of civilization received only diamonds and gold.

It might be that the valuables sought—gold or rubber or ivory or palm oil—lay outside the territory ceded by the treaty the bewildered native chieftain had signed or gained by rectification of frontiers and scientific expeditions. If so, one just pushed out and took the territory where the valuables lay. That is, one sent troops. If the natives occupying the territory resisted they were shot; if not, so much the better.

Let one illustration give the atmosphere of these proceedings. It is an oft-quoted incident, thus described by Leonard Woolf in his book, *Economic Imperialism* (pp. 47-48):

"In 1889 the British South Africa Company received a Royal Charter. The object of this joint-stock company, as defined in the Charter, was the acquisition and use of concessions in the country north of Bechuanaland and the South African Republic now known as Rhodesia. Its operations were controlled by Cecil Rhodes and his lieutenant, Dr. Jameson. A year after the grant of the charter the Company occupied Mashonaland with an armed force. Two years later Rhodes and Jameson raised an armed force for the invasion and occupation of Matabeleland. The terms of enlistment were significant: every trooper was to be entitled to choose for himself about nine square miles of the Matabeles' land, and to share the loot (i.e., the Matabeles' only property, cattle) with the Chartered Company. The Company then picked a quarrel with Lo Bengula, the Matabele king, and its mercenaries invaded his country and defeated him. By this conquest a joint stock company, situated at 2, London Wall Buildings, London, E.C. 2, claimed to become the absolute owner of 148,000 square miles of territory and 700,000 Africans situated between Latitude 16 and 22 south of the Equator."

In this wise Africa was farmed out to financial syndicates, which first were purely private, then semi-official, and then hardly distinguishable from government enterprises, by which time the territories covered by the charters were really colonies. And almost from the beginning these syndicates or chartered companies, since they were backed by important financial elements, had the support of their governments. In the race to stake out claims and extend them, governments therefore lent the full weight of their prestige and power. In other words, diplomacy entered. The period between 1880 and 1900 was one of ceaseless struggles over Africa. While rival expeditions raced frantically through the jungles to reach and claim strategic points first, rival foreign offices fought diplomatic battles in every European capital, with threats and counter-threats, alliances and counter-alliances, a whole library of agreements, treaties and conventions, a few of which were not violated, and deals whereby millions of hapless blacks on another continent were bartered away like so many pounds of rubber. France was arrayed against Italy, England against France, Germany against England, France against Germany, with regrouping in all the possible combinations of those hostilities according to the deal of the moment. Finally England and France in their struggle for the Nile Valley confronted each other in 1898 at Fashoda with swords drawn, and war was averted only by French retreat. After that African politics became a part of the larger European politics which reached a climax in 1914.

In North Africa, with Egypt, Tunis, Tripoli and Morocco, all countries of some stability, there was a different story, of course. There the technique employed was substantially that which we have seen in Asia: penetration through loans, intervention to safeguard loans, permanent occupation. Rulers were tempted to borrow, the financial rings of rival countries vying with each other in allurements; they borrowed at high rates of interest, and more than there was any prospect of their being able to repay in the condition of their countries; they borrowed still more to meet payments on principle and interest; they had to levy ruinous taxes on their already impoverished peasants to avoid default; internal disturbances occurred as a result of these exactions, and the orthodox chaos supervened, with the orthodox sequence of foreign intervention. It was so in Egypt, in Tunis, in Morocco, and more or less in Tripoli. And England got Egypt, France got Tunis and all of Morocco except the little that went to Spain, and Italy got Tripoli, though only after a rather inglorious war with crippled Turkey. The details vary, but the broad outlines are the same in each case. And in each case the series of events which concluded in intervention and could have no other conclusion was initiated by Europe.

Egypt, much the most important of the older African countries, had long been a Turkish dependency, ruled in the distant manner in which Oriental empires ruled dependencies. When Europe was awakening to its manifest destinies, Egypt's khedive was Ismail, a gentleman of excessive and expensive indulgences in the grand Oriental style. Obliging gentlemen from Europe stood ready to help him enjoy them. Money could be borrowed for the asking and the signing of tiresome documents. Ismail borrowed, and borrowed more, and then still more. Now, mark, the assets of Egypt and its fiscal condition were well known to the lenders and the governments which supported them. No English or French business house with similar assets could have borrowed at a bank. Egypt could, and was encouraged to, and so were Tunis and Morocco. The inference is plain. But it should be made clear that loans were contracted not only for personal extravagances but also for constructive purposes; for railways, roads and the like. But under certain conditions even productive improvements may be ruinous unless introduced gradually and over an extended period. They may create too much of an overhead for a country to carry. And with North Africa swarming with concession-mongers, it can be taken for granted that the last factor entering into consideration was the capacity of the native country to carry the cost of any improvement for which a loan was about to be made and a concession granted.

The Egyptian government continued to borrow, bleeding the fellahin more every year to pacify the European creditors. But Egypt drifted hopelessly into insolvency, and when its bankrupt state could no longer be concealed and default could not be avoided, an international commission was sent to look into Egyptian finances and make recommendations. What else could be recommended than an Anglo-French receivership? And there was a receivership. This affront to Egyptian nationalism, combined with resentment against oppressive taxation and misgovernment, produced disaffection, anti-foreignism and finally, in 1882, an outbreak in which many Europeans were killed. The British shelled Alexandria, landed troops—and have been there ever since.

The customary assurances of evacuation as soon as affairs were set in order were given by the British government, both to Egypt and the House of Commons. They always are. But England herself was the only tribunal of judgment as to when Egypt's affairs were in order, and that happy consummation always seemed to be a little in the future. In the meantime Evelyn Baring, later the famous Lord Cromer, was appointed high commissioner to set affairs in order, and he ruled Egypt for twenty-five years. It was in the name of Egypt also that Lord Kitchener conquered the Sudan. But Egypt, curiously, remained a Turkish province.

The last circumstance produced complications at the outbreak of the world war. They were solved by abrogating Turkish sovereignty and declaring Egypt a British protectorate. The Egyptians remained loyal during the war, took account of the rights of small nations and self-determination, and after the armistice prepared to receive their share of the millennium promised and about to be dispensed. The representatives they sent in the hope of seeing Woodrow Wilson were arrested. Serious revolts followed in Egypt, so serious that the British government yielded. Egypt was proclaimed independent, but with reservations. The reservations are: British garrisons remain in Egypt; Britain has the right to "protect" Egypt from foreign interference and the right to protect foreign minorities in Egypt; the Sudan remains a condominium, rule being vested in Britain and Egypt jointly, which in practice has meant British officials; and a British subject remains as commander of the independent British army. Otherwise Egypt is quite independent.

The world war effected one notable change in Africa. The Germans, of course, lost their colonies. Not as an indemnity, however. As it happened, while the peace conference was in session a British commission which had been investigating the administration of the German colonies in Africa made its report. The commission was shocked. It had found abuses— abuses of the natives. German colonial rule was harsh and immoral. The duty devolving upon the peace delegates therefore was plain. The German colonies were assigned—not annexed but assigned—as mandates. Not all went to England; only three-fourths, and by a coincidence just enough and so situated as to realize the dream of Cecil Rhodes and the early British efforts in Africa—unbroken communication from Cairo to the Cape. The rest went to France, with a little for Belgium.

Two exceptions have been noted to the general statement that Africa has been partitioned. These are Abyssinia and Liberia. Abyssinia, a black Christian monarchy on the East Coast with a romantic history, is legally independent, although it has been periodically under attack for forty years. Since Abyssinia soundly and humiliatingly thrashed an Italian army in 1895 it has been free of military threat. But its railways are foreign-owned, and periodically treaties have been concluded pledging the signatories to respect Abyssinia's integrity. Now this may be laid down as a law in international relations: when two strong nations bind each other to respect the sovereignty and integrity of a third nation much weaker, that third and weaker nation is about to go the way of all things mortal. When two or more Powers get ready to rend a helpless country, they always begin by guaranteeing its integrity. It should be said that Great Britain and Italy have just concluded a treaty pledging themselves to respect the integrity of Abyssinia. Disrespectful Abyssinians have denounced the treaty at Geneva and have voiced the belief that it includes secret provisions dividing Abyssinia into spheres of influence. Liberia, a black republic established by Negroes from the United States early in the nineteenth century, also is independent legally, but because of its origin is under American patronage and American advisers administer its affairs. This is, however, a distant patronage, and Liberia, having the good fortune to be relatively poor, has been left relatively free. But it appears to have been discovered that rubber can be grown in Liberia, and American patronage promises to be more cordial. American rubber interests already are supposed to have concessions there.

Africa, in short, can hardly be said to be even an appendage to Europe. It is in fact in bondage to Europe.

CHAPTER VII

REACTION: THE NATIVE WORM TURNS

IN the period before the world war, imperialism gave rise to only one major problem: which should be the biggest and richest empire? The only complications were those formed by the struggle between rival empires for the most valuable territories. But they were enough to set all Europe feverishly to arming, and to keep the continent tensed until the breaking point in 1914. It would be exaggerating to say that the world war was caused by imperialistic rivalries alone. European hatreds antedate the scramble for territorial possessions, and have vented themselves in bloodshed for purely local reasons, or for no reason at all. But more than any other influence the imperialistic rivalries served to bring about the array of hostile Powers in shifting balances and, later, armed camps, which made war the logical next step. They created issues which exacerbated existing hostilities where they did not create new hostilities. The undeveloped regions of the world were, as Walter Lippmann has called them, the stakes of diplomacy. As all modern history witnesses, "stakes of diplomacy" and "causes of war" are synonymous phrases. If they are not so in the beginning, there is always a point where the first becomes the second.

Evidence is not far to seek. It is found most cogently in the general atmosphere of Europe after 1870, but more specific citations come readily to mind. The Crimean War was fought over Turkey. England vetoed Russia's absorption of the Sultan's tottering empire and was supported by France. Not that there was any objection anywhere in Europe to the partition of Turkey, but no Power would permit any other to have Constantinople and command of the gateway to Asia. Even letting Turkey escape dismemberment was preferable. More than one weak country has escaped inviolate for the same reason. For such a country there is no surer safeguard of its continued existence than to be coveted by two or more stronger Powers jealous of each other.

Italy was drawn into its unnatural alliance with Germany and Austria-Hungary because of Tunis, which finally went to France, with England's support, despite Italy's large interests and larger ambitions there. How England and France came to the verge of war at Fashoda because each wanted an unbroken block of territory across Africa has already been told. Germany's encouragement of the Boers in their war with England dashed hopes of an Anglo-German understanding and materially contributed to starting the naval race which ended only at Scapa Flow. The clash of Russian and British ambitions in Asia led England to align itself with Japan by way of interposing a direct check on Russian encroachments, at least in the Far East. Japan, which had already come into conflict with Russia after the China-Japan war, was vitally menaced by Russia's fast maturing designs on Manchuria and Korea, and moreover had its own dream of paramount influence in China. Emboldened by the alliance with England, Japan took up Russia's challenge. The Russo-Japanese war followed.

Germany's belated but none the less vigorous entry into the race for imperial possessions and a place in the sun, and its very forceful emergence as England's competitor in world commerce and finance, especially in the Far East, threw France and England into each other's arms. For England and France crossed each other at fewer points than England and Germany; and Germany, moreover, was sharpening the age-old feud with France by obstructing French designs in North Africa. Twice in Morocco, in 1906 and 1911, there were international crises, with France and Germany confronting each other and England supporting France, and in 1911 all Europe appeared to be plunging into war. The despatch of the German gunboat Panther to Agadir in 1911 may be called a prelude to 1914. The conviction was stiffened throughout Europe that the Entente and the Teutonic alliance would have to fight it out. Finally there was the war between Turkey and Italy over

REACTION: THE NATIVE WORM TURNS

Tripoli in 1911, which helped precipitate the Balkan wars the following year, which in turn precipitated another European crisis. War was averted by the patched-up compromises reached in Sir Edward Grey's conferences in London, but the alignments revealed then foreordained the war.

Though it be anticipating somewhat, it should be added that the tension between the United States and Japan in recent years is imperialistic in origin. Exclusion of Japanese immigrants from the United States is only a surface irritation over an inner sore. The real point of infection is difference over China. Japan has evinced unmistakable intention of converting China into a province unless thwarted. And thus far it has been thwarted mainly by the United States, especially during and after the world war when European Powers with interests in China had their hands tied. America may have been pushed out into a position of protagonist of the West against Japan, despite its inconsiderable material interest in China, out of its diplomatic inexperience and ineptitude, or it may dimly feel that across the Pacific its own destiny lies; but in any case the fact is that Japan and the United States are arrayed against each other over China as clearly as Japan and Russia were twenty-five years ago.

To sum up, the disputes growing out of imperialism so charged the atmosphere of Europe that only a spark was needed to set it alight. The spark came at Serajevo. Until 1914 that was the chief historical significance of imperialism. And much would be revealed of the economics of imperialism if the balance were struck between the cost of any one of these wars and what the Powers fighting it have gained from their territorial possessions, including the addition to the national wealth accruing from the more rapid industrialization made possible at home. And this does not take into account the annual expenditures for maintaining military establishments and increasing them as international rancors are intensified. But such a calculation would be naïve, since it assumes that the profits of imperialism are as evenly distributed within the imperialistic country as are the costs of its wars, an assumption which will have to be examined when we come to ask whether imperialism pays and whom.

Meanwhile the lands and peoples serving as the stakes which were being played for in the game of diplomacy and finance remained just that—something to change hands according to the luck of the game and the skill of the player. That is, if there was conflict it was only among the conquerors. The conquered remained subdued. They were passive agents awaiting their fate, to be determined elsewhere and without regard to their interests, needs or welfare.

This is not to be taken as meaning that there was no protest. Protest was made, sometimes with vigor.

REACTION: THE NATIVE WORM TURNS

The Spanish colonies in America revolted, one after another, in the early nineteenth century and successfully, but they had been conquered in an earlier phase, and Spain's twilight as a world Power was already deepening. China, as we have seen, resisted several times, though in vain. In 1842 the British, in 1856-60 the British and French, in 1884 the French, in 1894 the Japanese, and in 1900 all the Powers had to resort to arms to maintain their position in China. The Sepoy Rebellion in India in 1857 amounted to a war in point of number of troops and money required, even if the end was never in doubt.

In Africa there was almost unbroken warfare between 1880 and 1900, but this was in the nature of "pacification" by "punitive expeditions." So many of these expeditions were despatched by Germany, Great Britain and France that they passed off almost without notice except, perhaps, by the thousands of Germans, Frenchmen and Englishmen left dead in the jungles, the German, French and English taxpayers, and the tens or hundreds of thousands of African natives killed or driven out of their homes. Three such conflicts, however, must be classified as full-fashioned wars: the Boer War, which cost Great Britain 30,000 men and more than a billion dollars; the Mahdist uprising in the Sudan, in which Gordon lost his life at Khartum in 1885 and which Kitchener succeeded in suppressing thirteen years later; and the war between Italy and Abyssinia, in which Italy suffered ignominious defeat at the Battle of Adowa in 1895.

Nor must it be forgotten that American troops were engaged for three years in putting down the rebellion in the Philippine Islands after the United States had bought the Islands from Spain without even consulting the Filipinos, who had joined in the war against Spain in the belief that they were fighting for their independence beside their deliverers. This was the war in which the United States evolved the strategy of the water cure for native ingratitude and discontent. Filipinos suspected of possessing information useful to the American army were pinioned and had water poured down their throats, one gallon after another, until they betrayed their comrades. Sometimes they burst.

There was resistance to the aggressions of the European Powers, but judging from the point of view of its immediate potentialities it was annoying rather than serious. It was instinctive, spontaneous and sporadic; provoked by resentment at alien intrusion or by abuses, rather than deriving from a collective consciousness of violation of rights. When natives were driven out of their homes or compelled to do hard labor for a less comfortable livelihood than they had had without working, or when they were goaded by general mistreatment and occasionally sheer cruelties, or when nations with a long history saw their cities swarming with arrogant foreigners and themselves forced to submit to alien authority, they struck out blindly. But it was an act of desperation, flaming out of unendurable provocation, and not an organized expression based on a conviction. Therein it differed from the kind of resistance we see now. And when punishment was visited on those who had rebelled, as it always was, they subsided into apathy. With repeated and forceful demonstrations of the futility of kicking against the pricks they subsided permanently.

The rule of the white man was accepted. After the turn of the century imperialism presented few difficulties to the empires so far as holding their possessions was concerned. The latter were resigned not only because they had learned the dire penalty of recalcitrance, but because they had come to take their position for granted. They accepted the status of inferiors, or, rather, took us at our own valuation as superiors. And had we not demonstrated our superiority? Were we not supermen? Not only could we summon prodigious armaments to punish the disobedience of men, but we had even subjugated nature. There was that in us which bent even the elements to our use.

We harnessed an iron cart containing a stove to a long string of carts, and bore men and the heaviest burdens a day's march in a few minutes. We spoke words into a small box and someone invisible and so far away that the shouts of a multitude could not reach him heard the words and answered. By ticking a small instrument we flashed messages along wires across a whole country. Our weapons killed men and razed cities miles distant. We willed a river to change its course and it changed. The rush of the mightiest flood was stemmed by the impediments we set up. The sweep of plagues was halted at our command. We could cut up a living man, take something out, sew him up again, and he lived and was better than ever. And our tools with one touch of the hand did the work of a hundred men. What could we not do? What obstacle could we not surmount? And what men could resist us if the very forces of nature could not? Clearly we were a race favored of the gods, and our rule over the animate and inanimate world was ordained of fate. To which men must bow.

So it was until recently. Then a change manifested itself; first imperceptible, then recognizable only to the discerning, and now obvious enough for the dullest bureaucrat to see that even if our superiority in certain material achievements is conceded, our right to impose our will is not—though the bureaucrat, closing his eyes, will not see. If we are children of the gods, the mood is to blasphemy. Resignation has passed. Our rule is being challenged everywhere, it no longer is accepted as in the nature of things. Our right must be demonstrated. And now rebellion is not a matter of hot impulses, unrestrained, unrecking of consequences and unplanned. It is a thing of reason and belief.

So our newspapers bear witness. And the agitation of our Foreign Offices and State Departments, and the dispersal of our fleets and marine battalions the world over offer corroboration.

The causes of this change, one of the profound facts of our times, I wish to analyze next.

CHAPTER VIII

SEEDS OF DISCONTENT

FIRST of all, there is history. There is the complex of forces rooted in the broader movements of our times. Foremost among these is nationalism. Not far behind is democracy.

Just what nationalism is has never been agreed upon by political and social scientists. Whether it is racial, cultural, historical, linguistic or ideological kinship that gives a group a consciousness of kind setting it off from other groups has never been determined. But the results of nationalism have been objective enough to need no interpretation and leave no ground for dispute. The crystallization of these groups and the expression of their consciousness of kind in desire for self-rule and of their consciousness of difference from other groups in attacking and being attacked by others—so the political chronicles since the French Revolution may be summarized in a sentence. The revolution of the South American colonies against Spain and of the Balkan provinces against Turkey, the movements of 1848 everywhere in Europe, and the unification of Germany and Italy were among the more significant outworkings of the principle of nationalism. And so is militant, aggressive patriotism. Whether it has been an influence for good or evil—in practice one's own is a virtue and another's, a German's or Hindu's, is a vice—nationalism has been one of the great driving forces of the last hundred and fifty years.

Democracy, though perhaps less dramatic and concentrated in its manifestation, has been even more far-reaching in influence. It is fashionable for the modern intellectual to sniff at democracy, and it may be that he is right. Whether he is or not does not concern us now. Democracy appears to be nevertheless a stage through which our societies have to pass. It may be just one more by-product of the industrial revolution. On the one hand, mechanization has given us widespread communication of ideas as well as large-scale production of goods. Cheap printing and newspapers have worked a ferment disruptive of all the established sanctities. On the other hand, mechanization by concentrating economic processes and financial control has put so tremendous a power into the hands of the few that some check by the masses was a matter of self-defense. Be that as it may, the demand of the unrespectable masses for a voice in government as an inalienable right has disturbed the smooth course of affairs throughout the Western world. The fact that the share of the masses in government has been almost exclusively vocal does not change the principle. The French and

American Revolutions loosed upon the world doctrines of equalitarianism destined to give some elements in it acute discomfort.

Now what reason was there to expect that the ideas of nationalism and democracy, though originating in the Occident and indigenous to its conditions, and no doubt intended by Occidentals to be confined to the Occident, would not spread? They were intrinsically infectious. They had universality of appeal. Why should they have stopped at arbitrary geographical boundaries?

If there were reasons why they should have, we took pains to see that they should not. For our irruption over the face of the earth was not only to get gold and diamonds and oil and rubber and high interest rates. It was also in order to do good. Was not ours the white man's burden? The white man, as I have already said, is a proselyting animal, with all the advantages of the temperament—these are patent and many—and with the compensating disadvantages as well. We, the Anglo-Saxons in particular, could not be content with acquisition alone. We had to combine acquisition with benefaction. That is, we had to stamp our mold on those unlike us. We could thus soothe our self-complacency, buttress our sense of superiority, and incidentally feel more righteous about the gold and diamonds and oil and rubber and high interest rates that we got. For were we not giving something in return, something, it is true, that cost us very little at the time, and how were we to know then that the time would come when it might cost us very much?

Our superiority was our justification for what we were doing. We had to demonstrate it to those over whom we were exercising the privileges of the superior. We had to show wherein superiority lay. So we brought young men of the races we were elevating to our own countries as students. For decades Japaneses, Chinese, Hindu, Turkish, Persian, Syrian and Egyptian students have been in our universities absorbing Western thought. In other words, we plunged them directly into the stream of our ideas and beliefs, just at the time when nationalism and democracy were dominant. Perhaps we could not have prevented these Orientals from coming in any case. But we did more. We actually channeled the stream directly to them. We started schools and colleges in their native lands, and sent our own teachers and textbooks, and taught our own subjects, our history, political science and law. And they learned.

Again the term "we" must be interpreted. It need not be said that the gentlemen at the seats of property and power who had solemnly warned that all this nonsense of public schools for the masses would only put notions into their heads and make them discontented—and never let it be forgotten that they were perfectly right—were not the gentlemen who started schools and colleges in Yokohama, Canton and Calcutta. In their clubs, their offices and some of their newspapers they warned again that this nonsense would only fill the native's head with half-baked notions about "rights" and unbalance him—that is, make him discontented with digging diamonds and tapping rubber trees for gentlemen in London, Berlin, Paris and New York. And again they were perfectly right. But the position of such gentlemen was delicate. They could not issue their warnings too publicly. They could not, on the one hand, explain away some of the more doubtful doings in Africa and Asia by saying that after all we were elevating the natives, and on the other hand, when those of a certain stoutness of idealism volunteered to contribute to that lofty mission by starting schools and hospitals, restrain them on the ground that it might give the natives a desire for equality and fit them to exercise it. When British opinion gagged at the taste of some of the African adventures Mr. Joseph Chamberlain, it will be remembered, answered that Great Britain was only doing its duty in the work of civilization of Africa. Could he, then, on behalf of the British government forbid Britons to teach the African natives to read and write, even if he knew, or Cecil Rhodes told him, that some day the natives would take to reading Magna Carta? Hardly. We have not all been stupid and unseeing. Most of us have been constrained by the nature of circumstances.

Further, there was the propagation of Christianity. For generations we have been sending missionaries all over the world to preach the gospel of Jesus Christ. Now, here in Europe and America, where we take our Christianity with common sense; where the tenet of peace on earth is expected to hold only when there are no enemies; where the doctrine that one cannot worship both God and Mammon is applied pro rata, six days Mammon, one day God; where the adjuration to turn the other cheek is obeyed only when there is nobody who dares to smite; and where we agree that blessed are the meek only if they inherit the earth—here Christianity raises no insuperable difficulties. We have learned to understand each other in these matters as practical men. But the black or brown or yellow man took his Christianity literally. It was given to him straight out of the Gospels, and without any of the unwritten interpretations we take for granted. And one hesitates to say it, but Christianity as it stands in the Gospels is the most subversive doctrine ever enunciated to mortal man. I use the word subversive now in its full Frank B. Kellogg-Winston Churchill sense, and not in its more vulgar connotation of belief in the right of trade unions to strike.

What did the heathen native gather from the gospel expounded to him by the missionary? The integrity of the soul as such; the universality of brotherhood; the fatherhood of God over all men, without reservations for black and brown and yellow; and the redemption of all men through Jesus. And in what specific doctrine of human relations does this principle issue? In the doctrine of equality, of course. So the native interpreted Christianity. And he believed that the Christians in Christian lands were Christian, and that if he and his fellow-countrymen became Christian the Christian order of things would be instituted among them. He set himself therefore to work for such an order. But how reconcile it with control of tariffs, grabbing of concessions, the opium traffic, "taxation" as an inducement to labor, and punitive expeditions? How reconcile equality, the equality of all men before God, with protectorates? He could not.

Since the anti-foreign disturbances have shaken China, it has been charged with great heat that the missionaries have been largely responsible, because they have stirred the Chinese with alien notions. I am afraid that is to a great extent true. It is true to the extent that the missionaries have been preaching Christianity. And Christianity is entirely incompatible with the foreign régime in effect in China since 1842.

Thus the concepts of nationalism and democracy have been carried throughout the world in channels we commanded. But they might have been carried anyway in channels we did not command. Among the major conquests of science over nature is the conquest of distance. Geographical barriers no longer exist. Not only are there facilities for the rapid transportation of men and goods but for the rapid communication of ideas. The conquest of distance made it possible to send instructions to an ambassador to demand concessions within twenty-four hours, and then to rush a military expedition in fast ships if the concession was not granted. But it also made possible the spread of thoughts which might be uncomfortable. And we made it certain when we established our settlements everywhere as little outposts of Western civilization from which Western influences automatically radiated.

Even if the natives did not read the newspapers we published or enter the libraries we opened in our settlements, they did come to work in our factories. They had to adapt themselves to new kinds of work, a new way of living, new habits, new beliefs. They felt new demands, acquired imperceptibly, almost unconsciously, a new outlook. They were broken from all their traditions and left open to the infiltration of other ideas, other motives, other values. Which of those more likely to enter than the ones current in the foreign communities in which they were living, especially since these were associated with power, wealth and prestige? And what more conspicuous among those ideas than nationalism, or the right of all peoples to self-rule and grandeur; and democracy, or the right of all peoples to equality and determination of their own destiny?

When in the early days our statesmen and their defenders justified imperialistic aggressions by saying that they were civilizing backward races, they were prophesying more cannily than they knew. They have succeeded far beyond their expectations or desires. Certainly the backward people have been advanced. For what we have achieved is this: we have fertilized the soil in which was to be planted the seed from which sprouted the shoot which hardened into the branch from which has been cut the club with which we are about to be clouted.

Nationalism took generative force from less abstract sources also. In the chronicle of the relations between the colored peoples and the white the year 1904 must be emphasized. It is one of the crucial turning points in modern times. In that year Japan went to war with Russia, and by the next year it had won. A great white Power, one of the greatest white Powers, one which even the British Empire feared, was challenged, defeated and humbled by a yellow people one-third as numerous, pinioned in a few small islands, and only one generation from feudalism. From Shanghai to Suez the whole of Asia was invigorated. It was thrilled by a new hope. For here was a miracle with material and substantial evidence. The supermen, conquerors of nature, whose slaves were the elements—they were vulnerable. Only the right weapons had to be chosen. Or, if no conclusions could be drawn, as the more balanced realized, at least a hypothesis could be set up. If one colossus could be overthrown, perhaps the others were not immovable. To be sure, this colossus that had been overthrown was hollow inside his massive frame, and his feet rested in clay. The Russians were fighting thousands of miles away from home with conscripts, at the best ignorant of whom they were fighting and why, and at the worst sullen out of long oppressions. And the war was directed on the Russian side by a bureaucracy paralyzed by inefficiency and sotted in corruption. The Russians defeated themselves as much as they were defeated by the Japanese. But if Russia was only a stuffed figure it was huge and impressive, and it had towered over Asia for generations. It was a symbol. And when it was shattered that which it had symbolized was shaken, too.

Here I wish to turn somewhat out of chronological order to cite a more recent event from which Eastern nationalism has taken impetus. This is the emancipation of Turkey. Since the middle of the eighteenth century European attrition had been wearing Turkey away. The successful revolt of its European provinces, repeated attacks by one European Power after another, especially Russia, and in one form or another had reduced it territorially. Financial bankruptcy and the resulting European receivership, followed by vigorous financial penetration by the imperial Powers, reduced it politically and morally. Then Turkey cast its lot with the Central Powers, and the Allied victory finished it altogether. Crushed and left prostrate, the Turkish delegation signed at Sèvres a treaty which left Turkey truncated and a vassal. The empire of the Grand Seigneur, one of the mightiest empires of all times, had passed. To make sure of the demise, the British incited the Greeks to occupy a large part of Turkey proper and then a joint Allied expedition took over Constantinople. The Defender of all Islamic Asia was no more.

A small remnant of insurgent Turks did not submit. Those who were not imprisoned by the British and exiled to Malta escaped to inner Anatolia and set about quietly organizing, announcing openly at the beginning that they would not recognize the Treaty of Sèvres. And they called themselves appropriately the Nationalists. Slowly they attracted to themselves the more adventurous spirits, their numbers increased, and when the Greeks weakened and were deserted by the British they leaped forward, evicted the Greeks, marched to the gates of Constantinople, and a few months later compelled the Allies to tear up the Treaty of Sèvres and draw up a new one. By the new treaty, the Treaty of

Lausanne signed in 1923, Turkey gained more than it had had before the war. Turkish soil was cleared of all invaders, the Capitulations were abolished, and foreign financial control was lifted. Save for the loss of its outlying and non-Turkish possessions, which the Nationalists renounced because—interestingly—they believed that imperialism was fatal and they would be destroyed if they tried to maintain an empire, Turkey came out of a lost war triumphant.

Now Turkey's astonishing recovery, the most astonishing in recent times, may be attributed partly to the personality of its leader, Mustapha Kemal, the most forceful personality arisen in Asia in centuries, and partly to the fact that England and France hated each other more than they coveted Turkey, and that Soviet Russia saw in Turkey a point at which England was vulnerable to attack— the same old Asiatic feud. So Kemal was helped by both the Russians and the French. But the rest of Asia did not go behind the records. It saw only that Turkey had won its independence standing in its own ruins, won it against the might of the triumphant Allied Powers. Asia had only another demonstration that the white man was not invincible, that his armor had not been forged by the gods. And the Turkish party that had proved his vulnerability was the Nationalist party. That demonstration has been graven deep in the mind of the East.

It has fortified the hypothesis set up by the Russo-Japanese War. The two together have given point to the intangible forces working through the Eastern mind—nationalism and democracy—and shown how they may be applied.

CHAPTER IX

SEEDS OF HATRED

I SAID in the beginning that I did not wish to discuss the moral aspects of imperialism, because I believed them to be irrelevant. I meant that no consideration of ethical values would affect our course as empires or our decision if empire were threatened. Great Britain will not release India, the United States will not release the Philippines, and all of us will not yield up our concessions in China because it can be demonstrated that it is morally wrong not to do so. In that sense the moral aspects of imperialism are irrelevant—that is, irrelevant as to us. But there are two parties to imperialism, the imperialist Power and the territorial possession. Considerations of right and wrong are far from irrelevant to those who believe themselves to have been wronged. To the contrary, they have helped form the state of mind of the subject peoples now. In that sense they are very vital to any discussion of imperialism. Our abuses have contributed to the change in attitude toward our rule and to the present status of conflict. The seeds we have sown in the soil we fertilized are the seeds of hatred.

What are these abuses? First and most obvious,

what may be called organized ill-treatment, the incidents of conquest. Invasion, bombardments of coast ports, excesses of punitive measures, seizure of land, forced labor or labor under oppressive conditions, humiliation of native governments, subversion of local authority, political domination and economic exploitation—all the concomitants of power exercised without check. From the horrors of the earliest Portuguese settlements in India which appalled St. Francis Xavier to the imprisonment of editors in Haiti it has always been the same, sometimes a little more restrained or more concealed but always the same. It could not be otherwise. As Leonard Woolf has said, it was not the atrocities that made the system but the system that made the atrocities.

There are abuses in another form, indirect and intangible, much less injurious and lasting than political and economic exploitation, but also far more provocative. Here it may be laid down dogmatically as unvarying law, a law fundamental in the relations of races, that you may subdue a race, exploit it, rob it, reduce it to serfdom, inflict tortures and kill, but if you leave it ground for self-respect you may escape retribution, you may even escape the desire for vengeance. That which strikes men in their vitals rankles less poisonously than that which touches them where they are only sensitive. This law the white man has violated wherever he has set foot. He has not even been aware of it. By unilateral adjudication a superior, he has been above regard for the sensibilities of those inferior to him because unlike him.

If as a white man, especially an Englishman or American, you walk down a street in any port in China or India (or Japan forty years ago before Japan had a big navy), and your way is impeded by a native who, being of a leisurely and inefficient race, ambles along slowly, what do you do? You boot him out of the path into the road. If he is elderly and recognizably not of the coolie class, you may only elbow him out of your way. But unless you are the exception, one of these sentimentalists who do not realize that the native must be kept in his place, you will do one or the other. If you enter a shop and the native clerk quotes a palpably inflated price because you are a foreigner—the system of *caveat emptor* still prevails in the old world, as it did here until not so long ago—what do you do? If your nerves happen to be frayed that day, as they so often are in an Eastern climate, you lean across the counter and box his ears. If at lunch your table-boy has forgotten to bring the condiments with the curry and the day is tryingly humid, you fling the water glass at his head. Say you are riding in a rickshaw, a conveyance like a barber's chair set on two high wheels and drawn by a man between shafts who runs at a steady trot for ten minutes or two hours. You have told him where to go—in English, of course, because you do not demean yourself by learning the native language. The coolie naturally does not understand English and takes the wrong turn. What do you do? You stretch forward and dig your toes into the small of his back. Or say you enter a crowded railway car and want a seat in a first-class compartment occupied by a Chinese merchant. You may either evict him outright or, if your manners are better, summon the native conductor and tell him to do so. He will. A foreigner wants the seat, he will tell his fellow-countryman. For he, too, has learned to take it as of Divine dispensation that the foreigner is king.

These are merely typical of a day's events anywhere in the East, so common as to pass unnoticed. They are typical incidents wherever the Anglo-Saxon rules men of another color. Sarah Gertrude Millin, in her book, "The South Africans," tells of Gandhi's first visit to South Africa. He had come to Durban from London, where he had been practising law. In Durban he went into court to try a case, wearing the Indian turban. He was ordered to remove the turban or leave the court. He left. Then he had to go to Pretoria to try a case. He took a seat in a first-class railway carriage and, when the other passengers objected to riding with an Indian, was ordered into the baggage car. Refusing to go he was put off the train. Later, arriving in Johannesburg and driving to a hotel, he was refused admittance because he was an Indian. And this was Gandhi! Mrs. Millin also tells of the arrival in South Africa of Gokhale, a Brahmin of the highest caste and a member of the Vice-regal Council in India. He had come to South Africa on a political mission, and when he went to make an official call was forced to climb several flights of stairs. In that building the orders were that no colored person was to be carried in the elevator.

The native who is booted into the street picks himself up, turns with a flush of anger, sees that it is a foreigner who has kicked him, swallows his wrath, and adds his humiliation to the plenteous store of philosophy his race has had occasion to acquire. What else is there to do? He cannot defend himself. He is racially old, of a stock no longer physically combative. He cannot yield to his impulses and plunge a knife into the throat or summon others to take mob vengeance, for he has learned the price exacted for such defiance of the fates. There is no recourse to any authority. His own people are powerless, and the foreign official who will or dares to discipline his own people for offenses against a native, thus shattering white solidarity, is so rare an exception that the appeal to foreign authority is scarcely worth making. (Where the natives have of late become so self-assertive as to be ominous, foreign authority is more cognizant of law and order.) What else, then, is there for the native to do but lay up against the foreigner and all of his blood a smouldering hatred and a score that must one day be settled?

Now not all the 400,000,000 Chinese, 350,000,000 Indians and 140,000,000 Africans have been kicked off the street or put off trains; but all have suffered blows more subtly administered and more painful and searing of memory. All have smarted under the mark of inferiority branded without discrimination and en masse. What this means in the concrete is best conveyed by actual incidents.

In Shanghai there is a park on the river front at the entrance to which there used to be a sign stating substantially that entry was forbidden to Chinese and dogs. The sign has since been removed as being too outspoken, but the prohibition is still in effect. No Chinese dare enter except as a gardener or a nurse to a white child. In Shanghai also there is a public recreation ground set aside for various foreign sports. These sacred precincts also no Chinese may invade. Once some years ago the officers of the American amateur baseball club thoughtlessly invited the baseball team of St. John's College, an American Episcopalian missionary institution, to a game with the American amateur team. The game was played in the recreation grounds. Furore followed. Formal protest was made to the American club, with a warning that if ever again those precincts were similarly defiled on its responsibility, even though by Chinese college boys in a Christian mission institution, the American club itself would be excluded. But Chinese are still admitted as coolies or as servants.

An experience of my own is even more to the point. I was seated at lunch one day in my hotel in Shanghai when a visiting card was brought to me. It was the card of the secretary to the president of the country, a young man I had come to know well in Peking. He was well educated, well bred, familiar with foreign usages from years in an American university, and a gentleman. I had him shown in and asked him to join me at lunch. After lunch we left together to pay a call. That evening I was formally waited upon by one of the managerial staff of the hotel, who informed me that the hotel's regulations forbade Chinese to eat in the public dining-room if wearing Chinese clothes. There was, however, a back room where foreign residents of the hotel could take their Chinese guests. My guest that day had worn Chinese clothes and had sat with me in the public dining-room. Would I please desist from the practice? I explained who my guest was. Nevertheless, he said, such were the regulations and they applied to all Chinese.

An American friend came to me one day in Peking in embarrassment. He had just had an awkward experience of which he wanted to unburden himself. Having but recently come to China, his imagination was still sensitive to impressions against which one comes later to harden oneself. It was one of Peking's relentless days, with winds swooping down from the Mongolian plains. My friend was in a rickshaw in the thoroughfare leading to the Peking Club, and was just turning into the gateway of the club compound when he was hailed from a rickshaw coming toward him. He recognized one of the executive heads of the Foreign Office, a Chinese educated at Cambridge, accustomed to being received in good society in the European capitals in which he had been stationed on diplomatic duty, a cosmopolitan and a gentleman. The Chinese wanted to communicate some news to my friend, who was a correspondent. They sat in their rickshaws in the bitter wind, both numb with cold. It was obvious that the American was about to go into the club. Why should he not ask the Chinese in for a few minutes, so that they could talk in comfort? Because the Chinese was a Chinese. And as a Chinese, though his might be the blood of Confucius, the intellect of an Aristotle, the graces of a Chesterfield and the position of president of his country, he could not pass over that threshold save as bar-boy to serve the foreigners their drinks. And they sat there, the one conscious of his rudeness though the guilt was not his, and the other conscious that the rudeness was more than personal, it was racial.

Throughout the East it has always been inexorable law that where the foreigner meets for social intercourse, though the place be semi-public as a club, there the native is proscribed, though it be in his own country and he of the highest official position, of the oldest aristocracy, and impeccable of manners, according to our code as well as his. For he is a native, nevertheless. Recently there has been a barely perceptible relaxation of the Medean law, especially where the native has become a little less self-abased. In Tokyo, for instance, the Japanese nobility may now mingle on equal terms in the Tokyo Club with British and American sales representatives. For Japan is a world Power, Tokyo is its capital, and diplomatic courtesies entail certain sacrifices. But not yet in Yokohama and Kobe, where the foreign commercial communities flourish. There the commercial men's society is still undefiled of descendants of *daimyos* whose lineage goes back thirty generations. There diplomatic courtesies impose no obligations, not even that of courtesy.

The tone of more intimate social relations can be imagined. Better to say there are no social relations. An invisible but for all practical purposes insurmountable barrier is set up, with a small alien minority on one side and the native race on the other. These are two separate worlds, touching each other in relations of buyer and seller, employer and employee, master and servant, or in the externals of formal official intercourse; but never truly meeting, never sharing any experience, and never understanding each other. The venturesome spirit among the newcomers who seeks to cross the barrier is regarded by his own people as a little "queer." And he becomes definitely suspect if, because his imagination is stirred by the glamor of an old, exotic civilization, or his sympathies are drawn to the people themselves or, just by chance, he establishes personal relations with them beyond the demands of his official duties or his business. He is considered somewhat disloyal, if not subversive of white prestige. And ostracism is his lot if he commits the ultimate blasphemy—if, that is, he marries a woman of the native race.

The young man may be of a middle-class family in an English provincial town who has come to the East to join the staff of a trading firm with the highly cerebral function of seeing that forms are properly filled out. He may be commonplace, dull, undereducated. The woman he marries may be the daughter of a Manchu prince, of the most distinguished Chinese philosopher of his generation, of a Japanese viscount of the ancient clans, or of a high-caste Brahmin. But in marrying her he has demeaned himself and betrayed his own people. He has lowered the white man's prestige. He is automatically and ipso facto ostracised and his children will be pariahs. His business associates may still speak to him, though a little distantly. If he is already a member of the club, his fellow-members may still drink with him. But he will not again be permitted to profane the middle-class English houses where once he was received.

In the Philippine Islands, for instance, a conspicuous outpost of democracy, what happens if the son of a Pennsylvania puddler, himself a salesman, is swept away by tropical passions and marries a Filipina? She may have been educated in Paris and Boston, in her veins may be mingled the blood of a Spanish aristocrat of pre-Columbus lineage, she may be a lady by any European standard. But she is thereafter cut by the wives of one-time retail grocers of the best Iowa and Kansas county-seat families. And the Filipino who has degrees from Harvard and the Sorbonne, into whose making have gone both Spanish and Anglo-Saxon cultures—will the brown of his skin ever cast a shadow on the pure white of the Elks Club, arbiter elegantiarum of American Manila? Hardly. The American clerk in the shop on the Escolta, that very apotheosis of Main Street, who has but recently been discharged from the ranks of the American army stationed in the Islands, cultivates soon enough a delicate eclecticism in social relationships. He cannot be asked to take his evening beer at the Elks Club bar by the side of one who is tainted with brown. Now, America's rule in the Philippines has been singularly decent. Since the bad faith by which the Islands were acquired and the excesses with which the Filipino revolt was suppressed, the United States has set in the Philippines a standard of colonial administration far beyond that of any other imperial Power. There has been a minimum of exploitation. We have sent more teachers than soldiers, and by self-denying ordinance have curbed private American greed, as the wrath of the Manila American against his weak government testifies. There are significant lapses of late, it is true. The Philippines government is being "taken out of business" and the way cleared for progress through private enterprise and control of such quasi-public activities as railroads. And the possibilities of rubber cultivation are intriguing, using the adjective with all its nuances. But thus far American rule has been without most of the abuses common everywhere else in Asia. Socially, however, we have taken over the worst vices of the white man elsewhere in Asia. We have erected a pale for the Filipino. And this is highly piquant to one who has been in Manila, observed the American community there, and reconstructed the social background of most of its members.

This social pale, with the insolence it implies and the arrogance it begets, is the background against which a race is expected to reconcile itself to alien rule. The spirit which is expressed in the pale is the spirit in which we have expected to win the loyalty of a subject nationality. Wherever we have failed, which is wherever we have tried, the explanation lies in this spirit and its expression as much as in any positive and tangible abuses. Now of course it matters much less to a Hindu, Burmese, Chinese, Filipino or Arab that he cannot join an international club in his own capital than that his country is governed from a city thousands of miles distant and economically exploited for the benefit of an alien minority. The one is superficial, trivial and transitory, the other fundamental, vital and lasting. He can be happy despite the one; the other binds him and his posterity in servitude. Yet I am convinced, for instance, that the mordant, deep-seated hatred of practically all educated Indians for England and the English is attributable less to the draining off of India's wealth by England than to the superciliousness of the typical Anglo-Indian, the scar laid on memory by some humiliation like Gandhi's in South Africa, and the never ending succession of small irritations to which every Indian is subject. I am certain that Chinese of all classes have not rallied to the insurgent nationalists out of any deep feeling over extraterritoriality, ostensibly the symbol of their cause. Why should they? Whether the few thousand foreigners in China are tried in their own courts or China's cannot strike very intimately in any Chinese. But every Chinese who has had enough contact with foreigners to be conscious of the foreign issue has had some experience such as I have narrated, or has felt the atmosphere in which such incidents are normal. The millions of Chinese in or near foreign concessions and settlements have known what it is every day of their lives to be under the stigma of the lesser breed. Of the Philippines I am sure it is equally true. I talked once in Manila with a Filipino with whom I was on terms of close friendship. When I had last seen him, a few years before, he had told me that he was entirely indifferent to the question of independence for the time, and he believed all other Filipinos were. They were satisfied with the status quo. When I saw him again—and by that time the Philippines were autonomous and American sovereignty meant little more than a governor-general and the American flag—he was among the leaders of the independence party.

"Don't give us independence if you don't want to," he said. "The decision is yours to make and we must resign ourselves if it is unfavorable. I can even sympathize with some of the reasons why it would be unwise. We aren't so badly off. There are no oppressions to complain of. We might be worse off independent. But you harp only on one thing, our 'unfitness.' We have come to hate that word. It is rasping to us now. It suggests a savage people come up for judgment before supermen."

This may not be rational. But men in the mass are never rational, and seldom so individually. Their actions always follow the prompting of emotions rather than reason. Why not? The responses of the emotions are surer, clearer and stronger. Reason gropes and is confused. Only by a long, sustained and orderly ratiocinative process can one emerge at a clear grasp of the meaning of concessions, loans conveying a mortgage on resources, treaties granting spheres. A Hindu must have a disciplined intellect and a knowledge of the more abstruse realms of economics before he can trace the influence of the flight of Indian wealth to England or of the tariff on India's home industries. Sovereignty is an idea, a symbol of a concept. The loss of sovereignty is indirect and abstract to the average man, and even to the intellectually conscious is felt only dimly and thrice removed. But a slap in the face is direct, concrete, and evokes response by reflex. And the outrage on pride from exclusion as something unclean, and from classification as of a lower order also needs no analysis in the recondite. These have produced a certain psychology in all peoples subject to them. It is an abnormal psychology, a state of mind in which long buried resentments, slowly accumulated antagonisms, and submerged hatreds override reason and sharpen every difference into a holy cause edged with the passions.

That is why extraterritoriality in China, equal representation on governing boards in India, and the American governor's veto power in the Philippines are all magnified into something far beyond their intrinsic merit. One need only talk to an Indian or Chinese student to see that more than a political question lies behind his almost hysterical and somewhat unreasonable nationalism, a nationalism which on analysis is found to be not so much love of his country as hate of its masters. It is against this background that we are now seeking to work out some compromise with these people, and because of it are finding compromise difficult. For now they are unwilling to discuss issues on their merits. They are unreasonable. But now we on our part are willing to be sweetly reasonable, in large measure because we realize we cannot help ourselves, and feel injured that we are not met in the same spirit. It could not be otherwise. The whole question of our relation with our subject nationalities has been taken out of the realm of reason. For that we have ourselves to thank. If our subject nationalities have elevated lesser resentments above more serious grievances, we, too, have jeopardized larger material interests to indulge smug and trivial racial vanities. The point is that the indulgence of our ego is one outstanding cause of the insecurity of our imperial position.

CHAPTER X

WHERE THE RACES MEET

I WISH to pursue the subject of the personal equation a little further. It plays so vital a part as to warrant detailed examination. I am not sure but that its part is decisive. Taking imperialism as an institution and an historical development, one must deal with impersonal forces which have given it foundation and direction. But since it is also a system of relations between men and men I am not sure but that the human element is the more important, and that a book which subordinated every other factor, while less logical as historical writing, would more faithfully portray what is happening within the imperialistic system and why.

How then explain the form which the personal equation has taken? Out of what reasons have we so conducted ourselves toward our subject nationalities as to engender hostilities beyond the necessities of attaining the objects for which we have subjected them? On general grounds, because we could. There was nothing to restrain us. Again it must be said, that the rule of men over men is never gentle and seldom decent. Men cannot be trusted with power over men.

THE WHITE MAN'S DILEMMA

Endowed with power and unchecked in its exercise they will abuse it. They will abuse it in ways not essential to the purpose for which they want power. This may be an unpleasant truth, but in the present stage of evolution it must be accepted as a basic premise in the relations of human beings, whether as races, nations or classes.

There are specific reasons as well. The conditions under which we have to live among our subject nationalities are peculiarly trying. With but a few exceptions, all our dependencies are in latitudes and climates for which the white man in unfitted. Almost nowhere in Asia, Africa or Oceania can he live without physical discomfort if not actual danger to his health. He becomes enervated, suffers minor disorders, and is subject always to serious diseases like dysentery and cholera. Few men who have resided as long as ten years in the East or in Africa have escaped some impairment in health, if only in lowered vitality and an overwrought nervous system. Digestive disorders alone are so frequent as to create an almost pathological condition. The white man on his side also is in an abnormal mental state.

The difficulties attributable to geographical setting and climate are accentuated by man-made environment. Sanitation, for one thing, or lack of sanitation. There are no sewers. Sewage is disposed of by strewing it on the fields. What this means in the routine of daily living one cannot understand who has come to accept open plumbing as one of the fixed properties in the scheme of things. American exaltation of the bathroom may bespeak a low ideal, but the saving of the senses makes for more than physical comfort. For those whose senses have been sheltered from birth it is indispensable to psychic equilibrium. All foods are poisonous unless boiled, and then are limited in variety. Is it earthly to ascribe social and political consequences to deprivation of milk, unboiled water, green vegetables and nearly all fresh fruits, to a limited and monotonous diet and the exactions of hypochondriac vigilance in what one eats? An army fights on its belly. Peace of soul rests no less on the same organ.

Cleanliness is unknown. It is not counted as a good. Filth abounds everywhere. (No more than it did among us six generations ago, but this generation is conditioned by the habits acquired in its own generation. There is such a thing as race memory, but it does not extend to external habits.) The evidences of diseases, some loathsome, are never out of sight. Streets reek. Back of one's office, equipped with all the modern, glittering and opulent apparatus of business system and efficiency, is stench. I do not want to overdignify the place of cleanliness in the scale of values. It is not among the absolutes. Athens was dirtier than Detroit, Elizabethan London than Indianapolis. I myself do not even rate it as a good. I believe it to be something apart from the cultural, moral and social values. But I find its lack wretchedly uncomfortable, I can never be unconscious that it is lacking, and I know that its lack affects me in more ways than the physical. Every individual has given hostages to the environment in which he was born. Only by a conscious effort of the intellect and imagination have I brought myself to understand that it is immaterial whether a race is clean, and that cleanliness has no relation to civilization. But living in a society which does not value cleanliness is hard.

Yet the physical aspects of environment are the easiest for the alien white man to adjust himself to. Far more difficult are social aspects, the differences in habits, customs, manners, values, ideas, and intellectual and spiritual outlook. Difference of language alone is an insuperable barrier to understanding and a festering irritant. Take the handkerchief. What an agency of harmony is its use, and of friction its disuse! And yet only a people schooled to sanitary practices avail themselves of it for its primary purpose. Consider thirty-six hours in a crowded railway compartment with those who do not. Position and gestures at the table, ways of conveying food into the mouth and the volume of accompanying sounds, if unlike your own, can inflame the passions. Certainly they can set up barriers. You can't eat with them, they're pigs, we say, meaning they don't eat as we do. If they be not so to me, what care I how endurable they be to themselves, states a position of unimpeachable psychological validity; but it makes for friction if you have to live with the people. The cumulative annoyances of doing business with men whose procedure is reversed in everything, who precede an agreement on the price of a box of matches with an elaborate duello of bargaining, who are dilatory and without sense of time, who promise to repair a lock on Monday and come Wednesday and don't know why it matters—these exercise a slow attrition on patience, nerves and temper. Nothing can be taken for granted as understood, in no transaction can it be assumed that there is only one way, in everything there must be new adjustments. It is like having to learn over again every day how to put on your shoes.

The necessity of ever adapting oneself not only to new and alien customs and habits but most of the time to conflicting customs and habits, imposes a strain which is never relaxed. I do not believe there has ever been a white man in the East who has not at least once had to curb himself by sheer will power on the brink of hysteria, who has not sometimes felt surging in him a hot passion to lay about him with violence, cutting down what comes within reach. Hence the booting off the street and the desire to shield oneself as much as possible by insulation, socially and personally, from the native peoples and their life, unless one is the exception, unless one is restrained by a regard for the integrity of the individual, and by reasoning faculties which have already brought one to understand that the factors of irritation are inherent in the situation and that the differences out of which they arise run in both directions: it is just as far from Calais to Dover as from Dover to Calais.

The element of strain lies, briefly, in difference. For the same reason life in New York is trying to a Viennese or a Parisian, though in lesser degree because there is less that is incompatible in the environments of Europe and America. For that matter, life can be trying in London to an Englishman and in New York to an American. Every subway crush is an incitation to sadism. But the Viennese in New York gives to the strain. He has to. Or he goes home. And the New Yorker who has had the door of a subway express slammed in his face on a hot day does not cuff the guard. If he did, he would be soundly thrashed or find himself in a police station. He has learned tolerance by observation of the price of intolerance. But in China or India or Korea intolerance incurs no penalty. Its privileges may be enjoyed with impunity.

Another factor in the personal equation, a factor of higher power, is one into which the physical or social environment and the racial characteristics of the subject nationalities do not enter. It is constituted of the racial characteristics of the ruling peoples. (I am not now indulging in the latter-day pleasure of tossing off biological truths; these are no doubt artificially acquired characteristics.) Which are these ruling races? British and American, in the majority. It is true that the French and Russian colonial empires are larger in area than America's, and that the Portuguese and Belgian are as large, both the latter having extensive holdings in Africa. But the Americans are more widely spread and in more strategic territories. The British and Americans together set the note in imperialism, the dominant note being British. It is not only that the Anglo-Saxon race considers itself superior. All races do that. But the Anglo-Saxon actually holds all others to be of a different and lower species. It is one of his foundation beliefs, bred deep into the unconscious. And as between Latins, Slavs and Scandinavians on the one hand, and what may be called natives on the other, there is difference only in degree. I was in the East when America joined the world war. Soon after, it will be remembered, there were subterranean reports that France was weakening, Russia was dropping out, and Italy was catastrophically defeated on the Piave.

"Let them quit," a British friend told me. "What does it matter now that America is in? Let all the half-castes quit and we white men will lick the Huns ourselves."

In form the statement may have been hyperbolical, in essence it is the conviction of the majority of Englishmen, although in emotionally less expansive times there might be mental reservations with regard to Americans, Canadians, Australians, and other colonials. And the conviction is shared by the majority of Americans. If this is how they look upon Frenchmen, Italians, Germans, Russians and Swiss, how may they be expected to look upon Negroes, Chinese, Japanese, Hindus, Filipinos, Turks, Mexicans—niggers in short? And how may they be expected to treat them? As they do.

Consider one revealing circumstance. Revolt against domination by the great Powers is found everywhere, either outspoken or repressed, as I have said. But nowhere else is it so virulent, so underlain with passion, so crossed with unreasoning emotionalism, as in territories ruled by the Anglo-Saxon. Why? Not because of greater oppressions. In fairness it must be said that politically, in what may be called public and official relations, Anglo-Saxon rule over dependencies is exercised with a greater degree of fairness and a higher sense of the welfare of the people ruled. One need only compare French Indo-China and Burma, or the Philippines and Java. There have been abuses wherever the white man has established himself by force, the lot of the dependent peoples has nowhere been a happy one. But I believe there have been fewer positive abuses where the Anglo-Saxon is the governing power. The British have taken, but they also have given in return. Even in India the devotion of hundreds of British civil servants under appalling conditions to measures for alleviating native hardships, measures from which the British cannot profit, lends a touch of fineness to an otherwise sordid and depressing business.

Why, then, this contrast in results? Why does the Tonkinese under the French or the Javanese under the Dutch, though exploited more than the Hindu under the British, feel so much less rancorously? Why is his disaffection so much more a matter of intellectual conviction than of passion? In Shanghai, in recent years the setting of the sharpest conflicts between foreigners and Chinese, when the International Settlement, which is in effect British, is barricaded and martial law is declared and troops patrol the streets with bayonets fixed, the French Concession, a stone's throw distant, is relatively calm and goes about its business unruffled. The banners borne by the Chinese processions all flaunt only anti-British legends. Why?

The personal equation. A Frenchman in Saigon does not regard it as an offense against his God if a high-born brown or yellow woman is seated next him at luncheon. He would ride with Gandhi in the same railway compartment. Frenchmen and Belgians and Russians take brown or yellow women to wife with or without benefit of clergy—as do British in Burma, Americans in the Philippines, and both in China and Japan. But the interior of the Frenchman's house does not thenceforth become leprous to other Frenchmen's or Dutchmen's or Belgians' or Russians' wives. In Java families founded by mixed marriages are in what American newspapers call society. Indeed, men of mixed blood, white and brown, have held high offices in Amsterdam and The Hague. The fact of their origin is neither paraded nor concealed. Nothing is made of it. It is just taken for granted. I was in Constantinople once when an American Negro professional dancer appeared in one of the Taxim night cafés with a white woman as partner. She was a Frenchwoman, as I remember, although I am not certain. Did the French and Italian officers and civilians present consider that their national and racial honor had to be vindicated? They took no notice. But the British and Americans! Their honor had been sullied. The British looked to the Americans to purge the stain and the Americans did. Led by a young gentleman from Mississippi, as I remember, they ordered the Negro to leave the place at once or they would bash his head in, and, further, to clear out of Constantinople within forty-eight hours or they would bash his head in anyway. He did. But need one go for evidence to the far places where standards depreciate? In fashionable restaurants on the Boulevard des Italiens may one not see Negroes from Georgia dining with eminently respectable and entirely sane Parisians? In short, it is possible to be ruled by a Frenchman, Dutchman, Belgian or Russian and, though misruled, to maintain one's self-respect.

I have been generalizing. It need not be said that there are exceptions. Not all Anglo-Saxons are bigoted and insular, not even those who reside overseas. Many have imagination and sensibilities and comport themselves accordingly, in China, India, the Philippines or South Africa as in London or New York. They attune themselves to the spirit of the civilization in which they find themselves, make themselves scholars in its language, authorities in its politics and sociology, connoisseurs of its arts. In mind and spirit they are enriched by the wider range of their experience, as is reflected in their attitude toward the alien people among whom they live and their relations with them. But such individuals are proportionately too few and too unaggressive by temperament to have much influence; they can only abstain from the general practices of their fellow-countrymen. It is the majority who set the tone and determine the relations between foreigner and native, and with them only we are concerned.

Who are they? Of what sort are those who go to the far parts of the earth to live in what they magniloquently describe in after-dinner speeches as the furthest outposts of their own country's civilization? Commonly they are supposed to be, and a priori they ought to be, the products of a natural selection—the most adventurous of the race, the spirited minority who gird at the dullness and tameness and monotony of home and prosy everyday tasks, their eyes on the dim and distant horizon, imagination aflame with the call of the unknown and exotic. It is romantic and a delusion. In sad reality they are, in intelligence, imagination and receptiveness, more likely to be below the average of the plodding, home-staying, 9-to-5-Saturdays-9-to-1 clerk, department manager, salesman or credit representative. They are commonplace, conventional, more deeply grooved in routine than their relatives at home; and their lives are no more exciting, no more varied and no more dangerous—again excepting men like officers on the Indian frontiers, colonial administrators alone among hostile tribes, engineers remote from trading centers, and missionaries on lonely interior stations a week's journey from the nearest white man. No small town in the Mississippi Valley or Lancashire is more dull, stodgy, mediocre or ugly than the foreign outport in the East. It is the ambition of foreigners in such outports that none should be. Put ten Englishmen from a provincial town and ten Americans from the Middle West in Bokhara or Bagdad, Peking or Samarkand, and they will set themselves vigorously and deliberately to reproducing, as far as physical conditions permit, the atmosphere and physical properties of their native provincial town. They usually succeed. And whereas at home, where things do happen, it would not be physically possible to shield themselves against the impact of some new impression or idea, living in their insulated and inbred communities far from home they manage quite successfully to do so.

More concretely, our representatives in our imperial possessions fall into three classes, diplomats, missionaries and business men. Diplomats are explained by their title. They are well-born, of influential family, endowed with substantial private incomes and social graces, and they have not very much to do. Little more is to be said about them, unless they are the rare exception, in which case they make history. The American diplomat varies somewhat from the type, but less than he used to. Formerly he was usually a wholesale shoe manufacturer emeritus who had been generous to his party's campaign fund, or perhaps a rather harmless literary man. Now the tendency is to make our diplomats men "of career," which means that they have been professionally trained in the State Department. The new American diplomat therefore is a Harvard man, he is at least one generation from the ancestor who made all the money, and his manners are un-Americanly good if somewhat self-conscious. Again with exceptions. But all diplomats are of machine-made uniformity in one respect. Their solution for all the problems of any country not a great Power is a Strong Man. It is their sovereign and only remedy for every ill, whether political, social, cultural or ethnic, and each one solemnly sets it down in his dispatches as if none had ever thought of it before.

Of missionaries it is less easy to write briefly. They constitute a strange and complicated phenomenon. But this surely is to be said about them: they at least give themselves for a cause, asking nothing for themselves except the satisfaction of seeing their cause prevail. Of few men anywhere can this be said, and of almost none in imperialist possessions except missionaries. Every missionary influence is exerted against exploitation of the native peoples by the missionary's countrymen, and in support of native aspirations to independence and equality. And the missionary has not set up the pale. Finally, his hospitals and his work of relief in flood and famine and plague have been of unmixed benefit.

The missionaries have high qualities but are limited. The limit is set by their occupation. Implicit in the very idea of missionary endeavor are bad taste, ignorance, impertinence, and vulgarity—spiritual vulgarity. It may be possible to justify religious proselyting among black savages, although even that is doubtful. But to go uninvited to "bring the light" to races which have had cultures, philosophies and systematized religions centuries before the Christian era, is justifiable on no ground. Consider the implications of the phrase, "to save the heathen." No educated man, no man who has read widely, experienced much, caught something of the color of the long procession of the race and the complexity of its history, seen his own knowledge in the perspective of the knowable, and the knowable in the perspective of the unknowable—no cultivated man can have the crude black-and-white certitudes which enable one to go out to impose his own cosmogony on another. He is restrained by his sense of comedy from the ludicrousness of so doing, by his taste from its crassness, and by his education from its presumptuousness. He is too uncertain of his own cosmogony. He is hesitant in comparing it with others. He knows that each must find the truth for himself and that what is truth to one may not be truth to another; that there is no absolute truth. Free movement and interchange of ideas and beliefs is one thing, but assumption that movement can be from only one direction is another. Presentation of one's beliefs on request is one thing; gratuitously thrusting them forward on the assumption that they are the only tenable beliefs is another.

The missionaries reflect in their persons the limitations which explain their choice of career. For the great majority, what I have just written is much too solemn. It takes them too seriously. To talk of cosmogonies in connection with most missionaries is comical. For most of them are just ignorant rustics who have "heard the call." What should they know of philosophy or comparative religion or taste? Of course they know nothing of the religious beliefs of the people they wish to convert. How should they? They know little enough of their own religion. They believe Christianity to be the aggregate of the dogma of the fundamentalist wing of their own denomination. They do not go out to preach Christianity. They go out to preach Southern Methodism or Northern Baptism or Cumberland Presbyterianism or whatever it happens to be. And of course no Protestant "worker in the vineyard" recognizes as Christian a native who has been converted to Christianity by Catholics, or vice versa, a fact which sorely puzzles all the natives.

Of the stuff of life in his own country the missionary knows little. He has seen it only in the even tenor of his small community, or from the shelter of his church circle if he was born in a larger community. And such he takes to be the norm. But "in the field" his view is less circumscribed and he cannot lodge himself automatically in shelter. He sees life in the raw. And applying the unreal standards he has brought with him he judges what he sees and finds it wanting, thus confirming the need for salvation on his precepts. The missionary devotes himself to the material as well as spiritual well-being of the people among whom he works. And he likes them, though with the patronizing inflection of the paternal; they are his charges, his to bring up. But by his very purpose he is precluded from respecting them. They are all candidates for salvation by him, worthy enough folk with good qualities but heathen, dwelling in darkness.

It is no longer customary to refer to the natives as heathen. Only a few years ago, however, I was in Korea for a month, most of the time residing in missionary compounds. I do not think I heard the Korean spoken of except as heathen more than six times. "How many schools are there in the town?" I would ask. "Four; two of our mission and two heathen." Many of the old practices are being abandoned now or veneered since a new element has entered the mission field, the minority to whom the generalizations I have made do not apply. This consists of college men and women whose Christianity has a distinct inflection of social service, if some of them may not be said to be social workers with a religious inflection. They are doctors and educators rather than expounders, and their faith is a little unstable if not suspect. They cannot preach fundamentalism, but neither do they preach modernism. They do not preach at all. They tend to evade. If not they are likely to be brought up for heresy trials, and the number expelled from the fold mounts steadily. A bitter conflict is now being waged within the mission field and the devil of higher criticism is being scourged. After all, the funds which support the missions are donated by those who stand by the old foundations. They want lost souls won to the Kingdom, not heathen bodies made sound by prophylaxis, and minds developed by the teaching of science and sociology and civics, by which enough persons have been ruined at home. It may be predicted that victory ultimately will perch on their banners, in which case the few ameliorative graces latterly lent to missionary work will be lost. Which may be regrettable, but is also logical and inevitable. For urbane tolerance and religious proselyting are mutually exclusive.

Yet the missionaries by comparison with the third group of foreigners, the business men, are intellectuals and persons of rare delicacy. And it is the business men with whom the native comes most closely into contact, and by whom the tone of the relations between native and foreigner is set. They can be characterized briefly as one cut below Babbitry. At home, except for the few executives of large banks or trading companies, they would have remained in provincial obscurity, on the lower rungs of the ladder of success, fulfilling their modest duties, taking their modest pleasures, and in fantasy anticipating the crowning of a life of high satisfactions by becoming a member of a business men's lunch club, if American, or a sporting club, if English. But in Turkey or Persia or India or China or the Philippines they become each a personage, since his chamber of commerce sends resolutions to Congress and Parliament, resolutions promptly noted in the newspapers; each is a little satrap with native minions who dare not say him nay; and something more besides, of still greater influence.

At this point a distinction must first be drawn between the English and Americans. The American may have a snobbish regard for success, material success; he talks intuitively of refrigerator kings and beef barons. But accustomed as he is to social flux, the upward and downward movement from class to class does not impress him very much, even in himself; or, if it does, then only as a symbol of success. It is too familiar a phenomenon in the United States. Every American knows that the Olympian banker is at most two generations removed from the one-button gallus. Most likely the banker wants everyone to know. Americans may give themselves the airs of Titans but not of patricians. They can make no social pretenses even to themselves. There is nothing to make pretense about. The best of us have been in overalls all too recently. And look at us now. What is there thrilling in that, except the size of the income tax? American snobbery is financial, not social, its touchstone success, not birth or breeding.

With the English it is different. The structure of English society is reared on a foundation of caste, and only in India is caste more rigid. If there has been some relaxation produced by the pressure of the war profiteer and the multitudinous nobility of Lloyd Georgian patent, it is only on the outer edges. The more clamorous and unregenerate of the Laborites tug at the pillars, but as yet in vain. The small minority of libertarians, fighters for lost causes, and the flower of English civilization if not of European civilization, have sought immemorially to shake it, also in vain. An Englishman still knows his place and keeps it. Almost by the cut of his boots it is proclaimed whether he is a gentleman. And if by some biological freak one finds himself endowed with the external markings of a gentleman, he dons boots that will make clear to all men his proper station, that he may himself feel more comfortable. For such has been Divine dispensation, that each shall have his place and keep it.

Take such an Englishman and put him somewhere in the East, where there are no fixities, where Divine planning is not so clearly manifested. The bonds of caste are suddenly struck off, and after he has regained a semblance of equilibrium he looks about. He finds himself free. To the American the only bonds of caste he knows are those which pay interest. When suddenly shackled by them—or unshackled, for that matter—it means very little to him except financially; it happens too often. But to an Englishman the event is nothing less than cosmically revolutionary. And he never quite regains his balance.

So it is with nine out of ten Englishmen in British possessions overseas. For only one in ten is to the manor born. What of the emancipated nine? Within a year they will have begun to act like Cecils, of course, or as they believe Cecils act. They assume the airs of dukes, not knowing that dukes do not carry ducal airs about. They give the impression that their afternoons had never before been spent out of St. James's, a quarter which they may have crossed in a bus. Toward their native servants their manner is that of blasé young noblemen toward their valets as pictured in the drawing-room comedies they have seen. In their ancestral homes there was probably one slavey. To one who relishes the comedy of existence, there is no more delicious spectacle than that of the middle-class English gone Mayfair in any port in the East.

Like all classic comedy, this has its poignant aspects. For here, more than in climate, lack of sanitation, diet and difference of habit and custom, lies the explanation of the provocation of the subject nationalities. Naturally one must impress the dignity of one's ducal position on the native above all. Shall one associate with him? Or not discipline him when irreverent? Shall one not generally make it clear to him that he is of the nether stratum? And there lies the root of discrimination, of the outrages on pride, the affronts to self-respect which now have repercussion in matters totally unrelated to the originating cause. For these, as I say, are the men who make the social atmosphere in the dependencies. It is comedy to witness, but may one day be tragic in actual consequence.

Such is the setting where the races meet. Now the

way to peace may be through mutual understanding, but it does not follow that the way to mutual understanding is through more intermingling of peoples. The evidence thus far appears to be to the contrary. The cross-roads of the earth are more likely to be centers of conflict, breeding-grounds of dissension, suspicion, mutual misunderstanding and dislike. The Middle Western American who never leaves his native county may never know anything about Japan, which is unfortunate. His brother who goes to Japan as the representative of a Chicago exporter will know a great deal but all that he knows will be wrong, which is even more unfortunate. Like all the Middle Western brothers in Yokohama, he will know that all Japanese males are dishonest and all Japanese females are prostitutes, that all Japanese are this and all Japanese are that. In China he will know that all Chinese steal and lie, are cowards, or are this or are that; in Constantinople that all Armenians are cheats, and all Turks honest but stupid. Whether in Singapore, Manila, Bombay, Bangkok, Bagdad or Mexico City, the Middle Western brothers of the world know all about "these people," they voice their knowledge in the same words, almost in the same intonations; and what they know is almost always wrong.

I had never been in the Near East until after I had lived some years in the Far East. While I had prepared myself by intensive reading before going to Constantinople, I knew little of the local atmosphere or conditions. In my first week there I talked at length with British and American civil and military officials, business men and "old residents." I found that for all I might learn from them I could have left after three days or never come at all. With two or three notable exceptions, they told me precisely what their counterparts would have told me in any port I knew in the Far East. If I met a British or American business man and asked what he thought of any question or event, after he began his sentence I could have finished it for him. I could have sat down and written off his whole stock of convictions and opinions about Turkey and its various races in his own words. While I have never been in Mexico City I am sure I can write down now what nine out of ten Americans there think about Mexico and the Mexicans.

There is what may be called the outport mind, the product of residence in semi-foreign ports, within a country and not yet of it. The outport mind follows the same pattern, no matter in what country or on which continent. It has been formed in the same mold. What do most of the residents of semi-foreign port towns of China know about the Chinese, in Constantinople about Turks, in Bombay about Indians, in Manila about Filipinos, in Mexico City about Mexicans? How can they know anything? They do not learn the language of the country. They have no normal, natural relations with the people of the country. Its history and traditions are almost a closed book to them. They seldom if ever leave their semi-foreign towns, or if they do they follow the paths beaten by other foreigners. All their experience and knowledge have been gained in their hybridized inbred ports. What they know they learned within four weeks of their arrival, from conversations in hotel lobbies and club lounges with other foreigners who learned what they know in the same way. The last source from which I should expect to draw a true understanding of Japan is the foreign quarter in Yokohama. I should be more distrustful of what I could learn about India from the English in Bombay or about China from the foreigner in Shanghai, than of what I could learn in New York.

This has one other serious aspect. It is through the eyes of men such as I have described that we see countries in which they live. It is they who make the official reports to our governments, who send the news dispatches to our newspapers, telegraph to banks and corporation directors about "conditions on the spot," and write to mission papers and lecture to church audiences while back on furlough from saving the heathen. What wonder that we see distant places and other races myopically?

The distorted view is on both sides, for the native, too, is in an artificial atmosphere, in a community which is neither native nor foreign. Between Yokohama and a Japanese village there is almost as much difference as between Yokohama and San Francisco. A Chinese peasant from the interior feels almost as alien in Hankow as an American. In such ports the native sees Western civilization at its worst, and foreigners under the least prepossessing conditions. Some subtle element of adulteration enters into the character of the native himself. Uprooted from his environment and traditions he loses what is best in his own civilization, and takes on what is worst in the foreign civilization that he sees about him. He becomes himself hybridized and abnormal. What more natural than that rancors should fester in such situations?

If thus we expect to attain understanding of one another and the peace that comes with understanding, then better to gird ourselves for trial by combat. Races can meet to mutual advantages and the enrichment of the world, no doubt; but only if they meet on a basis of mutual respect or without infringement of one another's self-respect. In other words, they must meet on a basis of equality. It is a counsel of perfection, carrying with it the prerequisite above all that the Anglo-Saxon must undergo subjective transformation. Even then, only individuals of the broadest sympathies and widest tolerance can be trusted to leave their native shores. To live among those whose background touches one's own at no point, whose values are in terms not even translatable in one's terms, is at best trying enough. And we have sent as our representatives to our subject nationalities the narrow, the intolerant and the insular, with results such as are already plain.

CHAPTER XI

TRUMPETS OF ARMAGEDDON

THE spirit of the times and the antagonisms we have fired are two underlying causes of the reaction of the subject nationalities against acceptance of European domination. A third cause, less deeply rooted but more immediately effective, is the world war. The disaster of the war was confined to Europe, but its repercussions were felt in the other continents more than is as yet even dimly realized by Western statesmen. For all men, not only Europeans and Americans, were the foundations shaken by those four years.

Throughout the period of rapid Western expansion in the last half of the nineteenth century, white solidarity was religiously maintained against those whom we overran. It was partly instinctive, out of the concept of our mission to bear the torch of civilization to the barbarian, and partly self-protective. We were invaders and among enemies, and, moreover, in the minority. At any rate, whatever our relations might be among ourselves, against the natives we had conquered our front was unbroken. The German might exert himself to bring confusion to

THE WHITE MAN'S DILEMMA

the Frenchman wherever they were in rivalry for the right of conquest. So, too, the Englishman and German, the Englishman and Frenchman, the Frenchman and Italian. But they were as one if either of them were challenged by the native. As individuals, British and Americans or British and Germans might open each other's heads in rows in hotel bars, but against the native they made common cause. "We whites must keep up our prestige," they said in one of the favorite outport phrases. On the whole, white solidarity did bolster up white prestige and lend color of reality to the assumption of white superiority which the conquered nations accepted no less than ourselves. Gods fall out only among themselves.

Not since the imperialistic era had begun had there been a general European war. Of such wars as there were came only echoes from afar, and then audible only to that infinitesimal minority which is aware of world affairs. Again I must point out the disadvantages that lay in the conquest of distance. The channels of communication could not be dammed up at will. It was now possible for the remotest people to get a glimpse of ourselves in natural behavior. If it was not, we made it not only possible but inescapable. We brought the war to the Hindu on the Ganges, the Chinese on the Yangtze, the Arab in the desert. We focussed it for him. The art of war had become refined. We fought in the air, under the sea, and in men's minds. And the propaganda arm was mighty in offense. By cable and wireless both sides sent news services gratis to all parts of the world, neutral or combatant. They provided newspapers with photographs made ready for reproduction, depicting their own chivalries and victories, the enemy's atrocities and defeats. If there were no newspapers they started them. In short, all the resources of propaganda were intensively employed.

The spectacle was not a very edifying one. Still less was it conducive to vindication of the belief that the white man was a superman, endowed with superior wisdom and Divinely elected for the mastery of the earth. If only half of what each side said of the other was true, both were bad enough. And we pointed the demonstration by bringing Africans, Indians, Arabs and Chinese into the war zones to kill Austrians and Germans, thus giving first-hand evidence that a white man could be laid low by a bullet fired from a weapon in a brown or black or yellow hand. And other white men not only incited the act but applauded its success. What price white solidarity then?

In the last war the whole world was a battlefield, for what place was so remote that it could not contribute some war material or food to the enemy? And could we not strike at the enemy as decisively through his commerce as in the trenches? It was imperative, therefore, to array on one's side every land and every people, however inconsequential in themselves. And since nearly all of them outside Europe had no concern with the quarrel in the first instance, it was imperative to persuade them that they had a grievance against the enemy. This was easy.

On the one side, through our far-reaching and efficient channels of propaganda, we showed the offenses committed by Germany against weaker nations. In Asia and Africa nothing could have been simpler. It was necessary only to reproduce pages out of any standard history. The evidence was in any library. We presented it effectively. Those against whom, as we have seen, the Germans had been guilty of encroachments pondered the evidence. While the educated minority had been aware of it all the time, now it was presented so the barely literate could understand, and even to the educated it now had the added force of corroboration by a third party. In short, they were convinced. Germany really was a brute Power.

The arm of propaganda could be employed on both sides, however. The Germans also used it to destructive purpose. They, too, had newspapers, news services, agents and pamphlet presses everywhere, especially in Asia, and more particularly where the British, French and Russians stood in the relation of conquerors. How far did the Germans have to seek for evidence? Since the Allied Powers had launched out on the career of imperialistic aggression earlier than Germany, it was easier for the Germans to find evidence than for the Allies. What fruitful material there was in England's record in China, India, Egypt, South Africa and Persia; in France's exploits in Indo-China, Siam, North and Central Africa; in Belgium's enterprise in the Congo, and Russia's giant tread over all Asia from Persia to the Pacific! The Germans, too, marshalled the evidence impressively. And then in the mind of the rudest native shopkeeper a connection of ideas was made. Both were right. Both sides had been brutes. And how villainously one's country had been dealt by! That conviction has not been erased and never will be.

The last war, further, is always to be distinguished from other wars. It was more than a struggle for supremacy between two coalitions. The defeat of the enemy was only a means to an end, a larger, nobler end. On the Allied side the end was compounded of idealism, democracy, rights of weak nations and small nations, self-determination, universal justice, and humanity generally. It may have been assumed as a matter of course that these lofty causes would be taken, like Christianity, with common sense, or at least that their application in the nature of things would be delimited to areas habituated to idealism, deserving of idealism, and, besides, well armed. But yet again there is the embarrassing fact that the flow of ideas cannot be arrested at points arbitrarily chosen by ourselves as the points beyond which such ideas prove uncomfortable. And so far from attempting to dam or deflect the flow we carried it forward on a tidal wave. Mr. George Creel's efficient bureau spread President Wilson's pronouncements to the furthermost parts of the earth as the aims of the Allies. A peasant on the Tibetan marches could not open a package of cigarettes without finding a neatly folded slip with the Fourteen Points set forth in his native language.

Now consider these aims and ideals as they presented themselves to a distant, neutral and unsophisticated reader, on their face and without subsequent emendations of the diplomatic Higher Criticism. Weak nations and small nations: what did those classifications fit better than China, India, Siam, Persia, Egypt, Morocco, Abyssinia, the Philippines, Haiti and Santo Domingo? Rights of small and weak nations: could there be a more cogent appeal to Chinese, Indians, Siamese, Persians, Egyptians, Moroccans, Abyssinians, Filipinos, Haitians and Santo Dominicans? Self-determination—the right to decide for oneself by whom one should be governed and how: could there be a more glowing promise? Democracy—the equality of all without regard to color, race or military strength: what more did such nations ask? Justice—fair dealing without regard to preponderance of power, and the cessation of conquest and exploitation by virtue of might: whose experience could have bred a more passionate longing for that than theirs? Here surely was millennium on the horizon.

Had not so many of the small and weak nations cast their lot with the Allies and thus been given a stake in the war, or had the Allies not won, consummation of the millennium would not have been awaited so eagerly and confidently, or its denial might have been attributed to the fates. But in the words of Edwin S. Montagu, British Secretary of State for India, in his report on the situation in India before the end of the war: "Attention [in India] is repeatedly being called to the fact that in Europe Britain is fighting on the side of liberty, and it is urged that Britain cannot deny to the people of India that for which she is herself fighting in Europe and in the fight for which she has been helped by Indian blood and treasure." The small and weak nations did cast their lot with the Allies and the Allies did win. The ideals were duly proclaimed—in words of treaties—but with China, India, Siam, Persia, Egypt, Morocco, Abyssinia, the Philippines, Haiti and Santo Domingo it was substantially as it had been before. There was only the one difference: an appetite had been whetted.

Again, the whole world being a battlefield, it was advantageous to strike the enemy wherever found. Not only must every country be arrayed against him, as I have already said, but he must be uprooted entirely. In the first place, only so could the distribution of the enemy's propaganda be checked, and the enemy's propaganda, as we have already seen, was highly embarrassing. In the second place, peace has its rivalries no less than war, and post-war contingencies could be foreseen in which it would be profitable to be without one's strongest competitor. In concrete diplomacy this strategy could be employed only by one side. German subjects had to be evicted wherever they had gained a foothold in Asia and Africa or the Oceanic Islands. The Germans could not retaliate, since all the world outside the area of Central Europe and Turkey had already been aligned against them or committed to neutrality.

Pressure of every kind was therefore brought to bear on all the outlying countries, especially those in which German commerce had been making frightening inroads in the decade before the war, to intern and then deport German and Austrian subjects. These countries, nearly all of them weak and small and non-white, might have been willing, although they had little positive urge to do so, but there were inhibitions born of tragic early experiences. Did not the slapping of a French face cost Algeria its independence? Had not the killing of one Englishman led to the opening of numerous ports in China to foreign trade, and the murder of two German missionaries cost China the better part of a province? Had not numerous punitive expeditions by every

European Power proved to the non-white nations the punishments visited upon blasphemies against God's chosen? The weak and small and imperialistically conquered nations were reluctant and fearful, notably China, which had suffered most from defiance of the fates and which was the subject of most pressure, for there German commerce had been particularly aggressive and particularly successful. But China had joined in the war on the side of the Allies and could hardly with logic and good grace hold out against the pressure. It consented, though with reluctance, and with trepidation carried out the decision. The Germans were rounded up, brought to the coast, and deported by Chinese troops. The deed was done. Profane hands had been laid upon the Divinely Elect. The Chinese waited tremulously for manifestation of Divine displeasure, waited for the thunderbolts to descend from on high. They waited. There were no thunderbolts; not one.

Here let it be added parenthetically that when the peace treaties were concluded, in the treaty between China and the Central Powers the latter had to forfeit the right of extraterritoriality, and none intervened in the name of white solidarity to insist that Europeans could not be subject to Chinese courts until China had set its house in order. Thus evidence was afforded that certain rights to white men were not inherent in the scheme of things.

Civilization, it will be remembered, was not secure

even after the armistice. One more peril was abroad, one more threat to humanity. I mean, of course, the Bolshevik Red Russian. The Red Russian also had to be isolated from humanity, especially in those parts of Asia where Russia had historically menaced humanity, as we have seen, and thus given concern in London. Again there was pressure to evict the Russian, and the most pressure in the Far East where he had been most menacing. Again China yielded, with reluctance and trepidation; could defiance go twice unpunished? The deed was done and again China awaited for Divine wrath to be visited and it was not. Nothing happened. A doubt insinuated itself. Could it be that not only was the white man mortal—it had already been shown that he could be killed by a shot fired by a black or brown or yellow hand—but that he could be booted about like a brown or black or yellow man? Was it just a matter of being strong enough to do the booting?

Thus yet another chain of ideas was linked. First we had convinced the weak and small nationalities subject to us that they had grievances against us; we proved it to them out of history. Then we gave them a desire for redress; promised it to them, in fact. Then we showed them that they might even move for redress by their own efforts; that they were not by any super-mundane dispensation estopped from taking measures in their own behalf against the white conqueror, for he did not appear to be under any super-mundane protection. Finally, the war had one more effect, which I wish only to touch on at this point. It left the great imperial Powers weakened, a fact soon observed by the subject nationalities of those Powers and not much sooner observed than acted upon.

CHAPTER XII

EFFICIENCY, PROGRESS, DISILLUSION

I HAVE said that the great Powers acquired and held empire by force of arms but that the task had been simplified by the belief in their superiority stamped on those they had conquered—the superiority of their civilization as shown in the stupendous material achievements of the West. I am trying now to analyze the causes of the change in attitude of the dependent peoples which has made the task less simple, which has, instead, raised a challenge to empire. To the causes already discussed must be added a robust skepticism with regard to the superiority of our civilization.

Among all the older peoples with a distinctive, highly organized society of their own there is disenchantment now with the marvels of Western mechanical civilization. A reaction has set in against the blind worship, the avid imitation and the gulping down of everything Western because it is Western, to which the younger generation of the East had given itself. Young men and women still come to our universities, adapt themselves to our ways and return home determined to apply the lessons they have learned. But they come now in a different spirit, not because only thus can one put oneself in step with progress, but because here can be mastered certain definite branches of knowledge and forms of technical skill. Their aim is not so much to be Westernized and to learn how to Westernize their own countries as to take from the West that which can be used to their purpose. It is with the critical senses alert that the East now approaches the West. There is a disposition to question the values in the conquest of nature, and to ask whether the "wonders of science" as best seen in an American city are as deep in meaning as glittering of surface, and whether they are worth the human cost.

The reaction was already noticeable before the world war, but by the war it was given impetus and articulation. For then the West was revealed naked of veneer and Western civilization appeared to have reached its logical culmination. Why wonder that the mood, now most dramatically expressed by Gandhi who would prohibit machinery entirely in India, should be so widespread among the older peoples, when our own literature of despair is so voluminous? There has been stock-taking also among ourselves, and many are asking whether the machine is the servant of man or man the slave of his own inanimate creation.

Almost every problem in the international relations of our time roots, nevertheless, in the Occidental dogma that mechanics is progress, efficiency the highest law of existence, Western civilization the only civilization, and resistance to our way of life unregenerate stupidity, obscurantism, recalcitrancy or impiety. This is the first premise of imperialism. The claims of an industrial system are paramount and cannot be denied. A society not organized so that the needs of an industrial system—our industrial system—can be met, must reorganize of its own volition or submit to management by those who can and will reorganize after our pattern. We go to spread civilization—that is, Western civilization—to spread it presumably where there has been no civilization before. The assumption, however, is one-sided, gratuitous, and subject to challenge.

Just what is the civilization of the West? What, concretely, does it signify? If the Western peoples were suddenly and miraculously removed from the planet or had never existed, what would be withdrawn out of life? What is it that distinguishes Western civilization from other civilizations? Science, of course; scientific discoveries and their application to production through inventions and machinery, and scientific method as the approach to knowledge. Science first and principally; secondarily, because abstract and of lesser influence in men's lives, Christianity. When these two are stated, the contribution of the Western world is stated; Western civilization is stated. All else—art, literature, codifications of conduct, philosophical systems—older cultures had too and have still. To none is it given to judge which is higher, theirs or ours. There is the distinction only of the prodigious material superstructure of steam and steel and electricity. This distinction and the ascendancy it confers date only from the industrial revolution, say a century and a half ago, a fact which must never be overlooked. Up to that time the white race, measured even by material standards, was backward. The splendor of the cities of the East dazzled European travelers in the Middle Ages. By comparison with them in such matters as roads, pavements, cleanliness, sanitation, imposing buildings, elegant shops and business organization, European cities were rude and primitive. It is not amiss to recall in passing that the span of life has been long, and that there is no reason why man and his works should be judged only from 1800 A.D. to 1927.

Of Christianity there is little to be said. The world has not yet known Christianity. It has known only Christendom. And of Christianity Christendom has made a profitable asset. Otherwise the Gospels of Jesus have left little impress on men's conduct, unless it be that out of the nominal adherence to them has slowly developed the dualism of conduct and profession which characterizes the Occidental beyond all other races and which those of other races brand too simply as hypocrisy. To the rigid and ungracious legalistic morality of the Hebrews, the

Gospels appended as a code of conduct a set of ideals of pure unworldly beauty, rarefied and elevated above the passions of earth, more sublime than those of any other faith. Their beauty has never been disputed by unbelievers, still less the desirability of their fulfillment. It has only been said of them that they were unattainable, a position difficult to confute. That the Christian ideals have never been put into practice goes without saying, and the Christian peoples have never pretended that they were being put into practice, or could be, or ought to be; in fact, any attempt to translate any one of the ideals into reality has always been suppressed and punished with all the organized force of society.

Nonetheless, Christians have always accounted it unto themselves for righteousness and taken it as mark of their superiority that they profess the Christian aspirations. Hence the missionary's disparagement of older Eastern faiths as unspiritual—they prescribe conduct which is attainable. The criterion is not what men practise or genuinely try to practise, but the sublimity of the ideals they write down. To Christendom therefore the profession of Christian ideals has served as acquittal of any obligation to act even remotely in accordance with them. Profession of ideals having been vocalized, men were free to prosecute worldly matters according to their worldly interest with a clear conscience. Asiatics and others of analytical bent, observing this dualism, have called it hypocrisy. They do not understand that ideals and conduct fall into two entirely disparate categories, overlapping nowhere, touching nowhere. There is, in consequence, nothing inconsistent in the same nations and social groups sending missionaries to preach the Gospels of Jesus, and merchants to sell opium, and battleships to enforce simultaneously and co-equally the rights of both.

Christianity has left one more impress on the conduct of Christendom. Taking the Hebrew-Christian ideology as a unity, as historically and theologically it should be taken, one may say that those who subscribe to it were the first to go out to murder and pillage in the name of God. The Hebrews, who went forth not to slay the Philistines for nationalistic reasons but in God's cause to subdue them that were against God, set a precedent which has been religiously followed ever since. The Moslems took over the inspiration and technique and may even have improved on them.

We may confine ourselves to science. Science is reality and the cultural deposit of the new world. But reduced to its application in mechanization and translated into the external and tangible things felt by the individual in his daily routine of living, what is science? The material structure is stupendous and its processes are gigantic, but put against it the question, To what end? Test it from the view that life values must be measured not only in size and volume but also in content. What is its meaning?

Imagine yourself seated in front of a convex disc which rests on a pedestal and is attached to a black box adorned with knobs, by your side an elderly, cultivated Hindu or Chinese or Persian or Korean, one new to mechanics and modernity, knowing only the tranquillity and leisureliness of the East, where time and space have not been annihilated by invention. Imagine yourself, as there issues from the disc a rendition in saxophone solo of a melodic confection by, say, Mr. Irving Berlin—imagine yourself trying to interpret to the elderly, cultivated Hindu or Chinese or Persian or Korean the significance of the radio and that solo; trying to make him understand the glory of the conquest over nature whose highest triumph is this, that through the atmosphere and across all space there might be brought to him and to you the strains of "What'll I Do?" Formulate the words with which you will explain to him why it was worth while pulling electricity out of the clouds and harnessing waterfalls, gridironing the fields with railway tracks and blackening the sky with smoke, making highways of the air and the bowels of the earth, penning up men in bleak factories away from sky and growing things, driving them at fiendish pressure in big industrial cities— why all this was worth while in order that you might hear a jazz tune transmitted through space. And then draft the answer you will make if he asks you: "But all these prodigious achievements, this harnessing of all nature to man's driving, the railroads and fast steamers and aeroplanes and high buildings, and now this climacteric miracle whereby man's voice can leap oceans and continents in converse—is this their fruit, the droning of a vulgar tune which I can hear every morning from the maid who cleans my hotel room?" When you have answered that question satisfactorily you have drawn the brief for progress.

Granted that the radio also brings rescue to sinking ships. Granted that it is still in its infancy and that it has wonderful potentialities and whatever else is granted to each new achievement of inventive genius. Yet the saxophone solo by radio is not so inaccurate a symbol of the results of progress. But it may be fairer to take the machine age at its highest. Let us take it according to our own valuations, as determined by our own choice of the boons we are most eager to hand on to others—universal education, sanitation, representative government, the press, all distinctive products of the machine age, all but sanitation existing purely by virtue of rapid communications.

Universal education, then. But where is there universal education? Where has there ever been universal education, or even education for the majority, or for more than an infinitesimal minority? I do not mean literacy, I am not confusing the two. There is no more fatuous and common fallacy in our thinking than that illiteracy and ignorance are synonymous, and that a man who cannot read and write cannot have more of wisdom, a surer perception of the relation of fundamentals, and a keener discrimination between truth and error than one who can read and write. No man could know an Oriental peasantry and suffer that delusion. Given a human situation, I should trust a group of illiterate Chinese rustics to find as intelligent a solution as a group of American undergraduates. I should not often be disappointed. I mean education, not literacy.

This that passes in America for education is only literacy. There is no education yet. Neither a science nor a philosophy has been worked out. One finds reading, writing, ciphering, the mechanical stuffing of a vast mass of facts unrelated to one another, and a rigid body of dogma forever indurating the mind against new ideas or a new outlook. Judged not by the complexity of its processes and the number of units handled in the machine but by the quality of the product, it is as a laboring of mountains. It has borne better bond salesmen, advertising writers and organizers. There is not much exaggeration in saying that the main result in America of the educational system, of the press, and of similar means of communication has been to facilitate the implanting of prejudice and the recruiting of popular bigotry, and to increase the striking power of the mob under incitation of shrewd and calculating leaders. If I were a Hindu Machiavelli with sinister designs for the control of my people, I should first introduce the Occidental educational system and establish a popular press. No other machines could so effectually facilitate the regimenting of the nation for my purpose. And I cannot say that I see any great cultural increment in taking the son of a peasant who holds a newspaper wrong side up, and at tremendous social cost teaching him to read Bernard Shaw, Bertrand Russell, John Dewey, Anatole France, Goethe, Aristotle and the Apostle Paul without understanding them, to read tabloid newspapers, success magazines and prosperity propaganda without understanding them, or to parrot glibly surface phrases out of the newest psychology, the drama, meretricious diets, patent religious cults, and the day's newspaper-made fad. Education is, no doubt, the highest good. A civilization in which the majority are educated will, no doubt, be the noblest known to man. But the machine age has yielded thus far only literacy.

The same principle applies to railways, steamships and other means of travel. Again it is necessary to judge not by complexity of process and quantity of units passing through the machine, but by the quality of the product. How are wisdom and enjoyment and the higher life proportional to distance covered and speed? The unseeing eye and the insensitive imagination comprehend as little in a hundred thousand miles as in a hundred. The seeing eye, the sensitive imagination and the pliant mind comprehend more in a hundred thousand miles than a hundred, but the wider range is not indispensable. It was not impossible to travel nor was communication non-existent before A.D. 1800. The difference is only in speed and ease. Does one who has visited a hundred cities understand them twenty times as well as one who has seen five? Consider the Sunday motorist or the American tourist abroad.

I need not carry out the same analysis and the same argument therefrom through the other variations on the theme of progress. With respect to the press, the same is true as of education. We now have news; the world is brought to the breakfast table. But what news, and put to what purpose? How is the harmony of the world enriched by the transmission across the seas of Mr. Hearst's animadversions on England and Japan, or a Japanese chauvinist's strictures on America? We now fly. We travel even faster than by railway or automobile, without asking why we need travel faster or whether we need travel at all. Flying, we can drop bombs over cities and write against the heavens the name of a new cigarette. We telephone and telegraph and use wireless to transmit what is taught in schools and printed in the newspapers, or what could without much loss to ourselves, society or evolution be sent by stage-coach post. We have multitudinous publishing organizations issuing between boards what is printed in the newspapers and magazines. We have representative government, whereby the suffrage of the people places in power the oligarchic groups who wielded it before representative government; if there is any difference it is that the oligarchy is plutocratic rather than blooded. We have neither greater depth nor greater variety nor subtler understanding nor wider play for the faculties. We have endless repetition, with bedazzling speed. I think this simile fitting as a comparison between life in the fifteenth century and life in the twentieth, or between the life of a modern native on the banks of the Ganges and the life of a modern native on either shore of the Atlantic. The Hindu on the Ganges describes a circle with a certain diameter and circumference slowly once and then dies. The New Yorker describes a circle with the same diameter and circumference many, many times very quickly and then dies. It is the same circle.

To the industrial system must be credited as beneficent the elevation of material standards. Sanitation, public cleanliness, the combating of disease by prevention and remedy, hospitals, control of epidemics, prevention of famine and flood, all have been made possible by industrialism. They could not exist without industrialism. Without high technological skill and complicated machinery there could not be sewers, and the character of modern life has been shaped by sewers more than by schools and churches. Not without point has it been said that the white race has surpassed others only in music and plumbing. I do not minimize what has been gained by plumbing, and by cleanliness and the conquest of disease. They constitute an unmixed good. The only question that may be raised against this good is whether too much cannot be paid for comfort, cleanliness and health.

Just as sanitation is a good, so is the larger production of wealth and the saving of labor by machinery. Not only the filth and squalor of the East are appalling; it shocks no less to see the tragic waste of time and labor and the pitifully small return. There is something unhuman at first in the sight of men drawing carts as draft animals, women bent under tortuous burdens, and little children plodding at the work-bench. Sixty coolies stagger back and forth a whole day carrying a load that an automobile truck could deliver in an hour. A farmer slaves all day in the field doing what an agricultural machine could do in thirty minutes. Housing is primitive. No American farmer who pays cursory heed to his agricultural journals quarters his poultry so meanly. Food is scant. For millions the line that shades off into starvation is always in sight. Formal amusements and organized opportunities for recreation are almost non-existent. There is only what can be drawn from one's own resources and nature. No automobiles, no schools, no telephones, no moving pictures, no electric lights, no libraries, no Y. M. C. A. gymnasiums, no vacuum sweepers, no canned foods or fireless cookers, no modern improvements at all.

You turn from this to a small town in the American Middle West and you find a new world, a visibly fairer world. Certainly the factory has created a standard of living undreamed of by even the possessing classes two centuries ago. What were exotic luxuries are now necessities even for the poor. Labor has been made physically easy and working hours are short. For the resulting leisure there is a multitude of employments. The slums have their moving picture theaters and radios, their running water and electric light. The ditch-digger can learn in the morning what was said by a statesman at the latest international conference, the statesman having had the newspaper reader in mind as he spoke; what the Prince of Wales wore at the Ascot race meeting and the provincial congressman's reflections on his four weeks' "study of conditions" in Europe. There are wealth and ease and comfort and a wide variety of interests. Is not the machine a gift of God? Truly is this not a better, higher, fuller life?

Materially, yes. In quantity of things possible of acquisition, undoubtedly. But one may legitimately question whether it is in yield of happiness. Now happiness is too intangible, too much a matter of definitions, for dogmatic statements or even fixed convictions. It is proper, however, to question whether the Oriental at his harsh labor and in his primitive home and without organized amusements or modern improvements does not derive as full a satisfaction as the American shopkeeper and factory worker. If he works hard and long, his work is not deadening. He is a craftsman, not a tender of machines. He makes something in which he can express himself. He does not spend his days turning one screw a thousand times an hour, always the same screw, the relation of which to the finished product he does not know or care to know. His pace is not forced by a thing of steel driven by a power he cannot see. He has a personal relation to his work, to his fellow-workers and to the product. He chats as he works, takes a cup of tea, stops to regard the passing excitement in the street, or to greet a friend or to reprimand his children, his workshop being also his home. If there is not so much leisure measured in hours, there is more of leisureliness. One does not see the harried, glowering look worn by faces in an American city street. Smiles come easily. All mankind is not ridden by the childish ideal of efficiency. The Oriental can play at his work, as Americans cannot; also he does not work at his play, as Americans do. He does not need a multitude of sensations to stimulate him or give him enjoyment. He takes his ease at a little tea-shop, listening to a professional tale-teller, or in the temple courtyard gossiping with his cronies. Nor does he have to make a vast expenditure of energy to maintain elaborate organizations needed to maintain other elaborate organizations needed to maintain other elaborate organizations that create an artificial demand for needless commodities—the complicated American game of playing house, that can be carried on without end only because everybody agrees to make believe as seriously as everybody else.

When one has seen the hamlet in which such a craftsman lives one has not seen every other city in his country, for not all have been modeled on the country's metropolis. Nor will one find him saying the same, doing the same, thinking the same, and feeling the same as every other human being in his land. He has not been regimented and his life has not been standardized, stratified, dulled, ironed out of every element of individuality until he is one pea in a huge globular pod, differing from the other peas in curvature, form and external variations but identical with them in flavor and texture. His life, in short, is not everything that life in America is, everything against which the rebellious element of the younger American generation inveighs so stridently.

These strictures are true but undeserved. They indict the wrong offender. The America of to-day—its monotony, tastelessness, vulgarity and mob dictatorship—is not the product of a unique race-stock or race-spirit. It is the product of the machine age, the inevitable product. America to-day is the England, Germany, France and Italy of fifty years from to-day. It is what it is fifty years before them because it did not have to overcome the arresting power of a long tradition and rooted social forms. Here mechanization could establish itself unresisted, and America is the machine age incarnate. You cannot have machinery without quantity production. You cannot have quantity production without standardization. You cannot have standardization of all material adjuncts of life without standardization of thought, opinion, conduct and morals—in this or any other continent. And thus, I think, may be explained in large measure the ill-feeling against America throughout Europe. For the stress of competition is beating Europe into Americanization, that is, mechanization; and since nothing is more precious to men collectively than their cultural integrity, against this Europe stridently inveighs. The spirit of America is conquering the world, the Europeans cry. They are wrong. It is the spirit of the machine. It is progress.

For the material benefits brought to mankind through industrialism there have been compensating evils. Every material good has had its price. The price may be too large for the good or it may not. Every individual will reach his own decision by his own method of argument and according to his own temperament. My own belief is that it may be too large. What has been paid for material benefits I

EFFICIENCY, PROGRESS, DISILLUSION

have been trying to suggest: absorption in quantity and size, outraging of instincts by the fierce drive of machinery, standardization, the drugging of personality, the dulling of beauty. If these were all, a good case might yet be made for industrialism. Tranquillity, too, has its price. It is possible to be too sentimental about the romantic and the picturesque. They carry with them poverty, superstition, subjection of women, a ruthless struggle for existence, enslavement of all the energies to meet elemental needs, expenditure of effort in mere physical drudgery, and a tragic human wastage by flood and famine and plague. Life in the industrially undeveloped lands is no elysium either. In favor of the industrial system there must be counted its potentialities; it is yet in its earliest stages. There is, however, a still greater price exacted by industrialism.

Modern science has affected life in two ways, in greater production of wealth by machinery and in greater destruction by war. The question may be raised in which it has been more efficient. Not only have there been created more instruments of war and each made more deadly, but the area of war has been extended and the advantage to be gained by war increased. Improvement in communications has made the whole world the stake of those who can marshal the heaviest array of force, and the machine has made force more destructive. The very newspaper records of the last few years are warrant for the question whether the one sure, clear outcome of the white man's discoveries in science will not be his extermination. The saturation point assuredly has been reached already. More, and the flood will engulf us. One more world war—if it comes it will of course be on a larger scale and more terrible in its destruction than the last—and the white race may be left a fragment huddled around its memories. There are potentialities in industrialism for greater good, as I have said; out of it may come a better, more scientific, and more rational ordering of human affairs and a liberation of energies from all lower forms of labor for finer pursuits. There are also the potentialities for armament and international conflict. It is not unfair to say that the first proceeds by arithmetic progression, the second by geometric progression. Is it unfair to say that, as world forces are driving now, the chances are even that the end will be suicide? This aspect is perhaps uppermost in the minds of the non-white peoples to-day. It is the aspect of Western civilization they fear most, for the menace stands out starkly, while the more speculative considerations with regard to its values are clouded and conflicting.

To the whole argument I have made, the obvious and most weighty retort is that it is academic and futile. There is nothing to argue about; the issue is in the past. Industrialism has come. Its march is irresistible, it is on the tides of evolution. There is no turning back ever, and comparisons are vain, whatever they may reveal. Other races have yielded in part; their industrialization goes on apace, the advance of its penetration visible from year to year and unobstructed save by the ultra-conservative and a few romantic Occidentals. They must yield altogether; if not willingly, then under coercion. And it will be willingly, for the temptations of wealth and comfort are too strong for any resistance which can be offered by yearnings for a legendary Golden Age. No race, as no individual, will choose poverty, discomfort and deprivation in obedience to a tenuous philosophy.

That may be. All the ponderables are on the side of mechanization, and the spirit of an age has seldom been denied. I am not sure, however, that the unindustrialized races can be coerced. Given a conviction on the part of their leaders that it is better to stand unreconstructed on their own civilizations, given enough Gandhis, their power of resistance is sturdier than is commonly believed, even if it be passive resistance, a form of resistance underestimated by Occidentals because repugnant to them temperamentally. A system of subtle, elusive sabotage could be devised that would nullify all the efforts of bankers, engineers, generals and heavy artillery, and make forcible industrialization from without so difficult as to be unprofitable.

When it is said, however, that the older civilizations must yield voluntarily or under coercion, a question is stated, not a conclusion. That question goes to the root of the matter. It implies an element of choice. There is a vast difference between adopting a new scheme of things on the belief that it is to one's interests and offers the highest satisfactions, and having to submit to the same scheme at alien dictation and for alien profit. In the first case the manner and pace at which the change is effected are determined by the nation itself, with such adjustments to its own traditions, habits and desires as will make the change easier, and with such ameliorations as are deemed necessary. Specifically this means that China and India and Turkey will be free to forestall the worst evils of exploitation of labor and natural resources for private profit. They will not have to pass through the whole cycle through which England and the United States have passed, but can profit by their experience. They can begin where industrialism is now in the West and not where it was in England a hundred years ago. In the second case, that of imposition from without, the exclusive determinant is the biggest immediate profit for the foreign exploiter without regard to social consequences in the country exploited. The desire for such profits is the originating motive of imperialistic expansion, and unless the change is effected under foreign direction the objects of imperialism are frustrated. Hence the importance of the question whether industrialism will come voluntarily or by compulsion.

The point is the element of doubt. It no longer

is taken for granted by the imperialistically dominated peoples that domination follows automatically from superiority in material development. So far as the future of imperialism is concerned, the point is crucial.

CHAPTER XIII

AMERICA GETS ITS STRIDE

AT this point I wish to introduce an interlude. I wish to discuss the United States. Thus far I have made only passing reference to America's part in imperialism. This has been out of no devotion to the American article of faith that America is distinguished by a purity of motive and idealism in conduct that set it off from the finite and peccant countries of Europe. It has been because the institution of imperialism developed independently of the United States, and the whole complex of issues with which we are dealing would have been formed if there had been no United States.

In the period of imperialistic expansion the United States was not yet a world Power. It was itself an unexploited continent, its energies inward-turned and absorbed in domestic exploitation. Gutting virgin forests, indifferent to future needs; constructing railroads on government land grants and procuring public utility franchises—concessions, in other words—from bribed officials or officials installed for the purpose, offered all the inducements of Africa and China in a pleasant climate and with the comforts of home.

America gave scope to many a Cecil Rhodes. And the natives made no resistance.

In the year 1927 no discussion of imperialism is complete that does not take into account America's recent acts and present tendencies. The energies of the American people are no longer absorbed in domestic development. They are no longer inward-turned. The continent is settled. Natural resources are already exploited or ear-marked for exploitation. Concessions are less easy to procure by the old methods, as the obstacles encountered by the giant power syndicates attest. Also most of them are already concentrated in a few hands. The key industries have all been organized and amalgamated under the sway of a few great concentrations of capital. Our productive capacity has outstripped consumption, despite the allurements and stimuli of advertising and high-power salesmanship, and we have a surplus to export. But by high productive efficiency and through the beneficence of a solicitously protective tariff, and by immunity from social legislation such as curbs genius and enterprise in European countries not so single-mindedly dedicated to prosperity, accumulations of capital grow ever larger. The law of diminishing returns has begun to operate. What might have been a long course was telescoped by the world war, and America now finds itself with a monopoly of the world's gold supply and almost a monopoly of credit. In 1914 the United States owed $5,000,-

000,000 abroad, against which it had invested there $2,500,000,000. In 1927 the world owes the United States $13,000,000,000 exclusive of war debts. The United States is a lending country with capital to export—to European countries at fixed and conventional rates of interest if necessary, to freer fields for pioneer and profitable endeavor by preference. America has swung into stride.

The first few timorous steps were taken before the close of the century. Historians are agreed that the frontier passed just before the '90's. Only a few years later America acquired its first overseas possession. The outward movement from the mainland began seriously just when the most radiant possibilities for investment at home became more elusive, when the trusts were all amalgamated or in process of amalgamation. It now is in full career. The drive has been in two directions. The first, taking propulsive force from Manifest Destiny, is westward across the Pacific. The second, drawn by interests growing naturally out of propinquity, is southward into Latin America and the Caribbean.

The *J'accuse* of the 100-per cent Japanese against America, varying verbally according to the individual, is this:

"We think of our security and at every point we find it menaced by America. We read your history and we understand. From the very beginning we see the westward course of your expansion. You started on a rock on the Atlantic coast. As soon as you found footing you faced west and moved forward, driving the Indians ahead of you or killing them. Before you had cleared the ground where you were you pushed on to the Mississippi. You found a pretext to attack Mexico, and after an unjust war of aggression seized what is now Texas, California, and other Western States. You planted your settlements on the Pacific coast and then, although you barred other countries from your continent by your Monroe Doctrine, reached out across the Pacific. You stretched into Asia. By a war supposedly for the liberation of Cuba, an island in the Atlantic, you wrested the Philippine Islands from Spain, at the other extremity of the Pacific. And now you are on the Asiatic continent itself. Under the guise of the Open Door policy you invade China economically, and while obstructing Japan and every other country, nominally as defenders of China's integrity are yourselves seeking by dollar diplomacy to reduce China to a colony. China is the next step in your westward progression, and all, like Japan, who resist must make way or be crushed."

It is the type thesis of the anti-American Japanese. While rhetorical, it rests on a substratum of fact. In broad outlines, if too accentuated, it is the story of American growth.

Unofficially Hawaii came under the American ægis long before San Francisco was more than a settlement. Early in the nineteenth century the nucleus of an American colony began to form: first the deposits of whaling vessels calling for supplies, then adventurous traders, then missionaries. The native population, Polynesians of physical beauty and subtropical languor, bathed, fished, plucked the trees of fruits, worked the soil desultorily for a few humble vegetables, sang, danced, fought occasionally, and were happy. Uninterested in the "future possibilities" of their islands, they were content to let the Americans, with a minority of English and later of Germans, spend themselves in strenuous work under a tropical sun. They were more content, since the foreigner was willing to advance gold on the signing of papers called mortgages. So, too, was the foreigner content; for the mortgages in the nature of things were all foreclosed, and in fifty years he owned most of the land and whatever else had tangible value in the Islands. On his land he was growing sugar and selling $10,000,000 worth a year to American consumers. As for the Hawaiians, they were Christianized and clothed by the missionary, taught to drink alcoholic liquor by the trader, and infected with syphilis and tuberculosis by civilization. They are now civilized and dying out. There were 130,000 of them in 1832, and 23,000 in 1920. It may have been a sound instinct that left them indifferent to future possibilities.

Three-quarters of the sugar lands being owned

by Americans, the direction of the gravitational pull on the Islands may be guessed. In 1875 a treaty between Hawaii and the United States provided for the admission of Hawaiian sugar into the United States duty free, whereas sugar from Cuba, a Spanish colony, was dutiable. But in 1890 the McKinley tariff bill removed the duty on all sugar and Hawaii lost its preference. The loss to American planters in Hawaii was estimated at $12,000,000 a year, a disaster which set in train a concatenation of events. I need not say that there was chaos, that law and order were jeopardized, that American lives and property had to be protected; and every American schoolboy knows that the Stars and Stripes now fly over the Hawaiian Islands.

Providence always intervenes fortuitously in such contingencies. Three years after the passage of the McKinley tariff bill Queen Liliuokalani, who had assimilated with her European education an attitude of patronage toward Americans, proclaimed a revision of the constitution curtailing the privileges of foreigners. Since she also had delusions of grandeur, she enlarged the prerogatives of the crown. The affront to democracy as well as to foreign property galvanized the American colony into forming a Committee of Public Safety for the protection of the rights of Hawaiians, who strangely seemed to care very little. The American Minister, on request of the Committee, asked an American cruiser to land

Marines for the security of law and order, which was really disturbed only by the American Committee. The troops landed and took over the public buildings. A provisional government was formed by the American Committee. Its first act as the government of Hawaii was to ask for annexation to the United States. To President Cleveland, who had just come into office, the procedure was a little too thick. He opposed annexation but was succeeded by President McKinley, whose party has traditionally a sturdier loyalty to the claims of prosperity. In 1898, as an incident of the Spanish-American War, the Hawaiian Islands were formally annexed to the United States.

Another incident of the war with Spain was the acquisition of the Philippine Islands. By the outraged it is asserted with some heat that Filipino aspirations to independence are the artificial creation of "professional agitators." Yet historical records show that there was a revolution against the Spanish as far back as 1790. There were others throughout the next hundred years, and while they were evoked by the oppressions of the Spanish governors and exploitation by the Catholic orders, they are witness to a sense of solidarity existing long before the advent of Manuel Quezon, Sergio Osmena, Manuel Roxas, and others suspect to the American raj. In the years immediately preceding the Spanish-American War a widespread movement had been organized by José

Rizal, national hero of the Filipinos, and Spanish tenancy would have been imperilled if there had been no war with America. Such serious proportions had this movement assumed that Admiral Dewey immediately on the outbreak of the war sent for Aguinaldo, the insurgent leader then in Singapore.

Aguinaldo was brought to Hongkong on an American gunboat and there urged by Admiral Dewey to press the military campaign against the Spanish forces. What else passed between them has never been agreed upon, but Filipino leaders interpreted it as a promise of independence. The insurgents proceeded on the understanding that they were equal partners in an alliance, assisting America to defeat its enemy and receiving their liberation in return. That they contributed their share to defeating Spain is attested by official American evidence.

"They looked on us as their liberators," Admiral Dewey testified before a committee of the United States Senate. "Up to the time the [American] army came he [Aguinaldo] did everything I requested. . . . I saw him almost daily. . . . I was waiting for troops to arrive and I thought the closer they [the Filipinos] invested the city the easier it would be when our troops arrived to march in. The Filipinos were our friends, assisting us; they were doing our work."

So successful were the Filipinos that when the American troops arrived the Spanish were penned up in Manila under siege. Essentially it was a Filipino victory. And the Spanish surrendered to the American forces with the firing of a few shots to save their face. Then the Americans marched their troops into Manila in a bloodless victory, leaving the Filipinos, who had borne the burden of battle, outside the city walls. The Spanish had so insisted.

When the war was over the Filipinos sent a delegate to the peace negotiations at Paris. He cooled his heels in anterooms while the United States was contracting the purchase of the Islands from Spain for $20,000,000, without so much as notification of the deal to Aguinaldo and his people, who had for consolation the assurance of President McKinley that he was acting in obedience to "the new duties and responsibilities which we must meet and discharge as becomes a great nation in whose growth and career from the beginning the Ruler of Nations has plainly written the high command and pledge of civilization." Subordinate to divine command was "the commercial opportunity to which American statesmanship cannot be indifferent." Both citations are from President McKinley's instructions to his peace commissioners. The undisseverable relation of God and prosperity is of pre-Coolidgean establishment, it will be seen.

Meanwhile the American force of occupation was inside Manila, the Filipino insurgent army just outside, their outposts face to face. Just how it happened has never been clearly brought out, and since it was inevitable the reason is immaterial. There was a misunderstanding between opposing sentries and shots were fired. Aguinaldo expressed his regrets and asked for the suspension of hostilities, but the American command had smelled blood. The order was given to attack, 3,000 Filipinos were killed in a day's battle, and a three years' war was begun. The barbarities with which the war was prosecuted shocked influential sections of American opinion. Mention has already been made of the water cure. Official inquiry brought out stories of the ruthless slaughtering of prisoners and non-combatants. In Mark Twain's Autobiography may be found his philippic on the communiqué announcing a victory in an engagement in which American troops perched on the rim of a crater fired down into the bowl until the hundreds of native insurgents who had taken refuge there with their women and children were left dead, dying or wounded. In this manner America shouldered its portion of the white man's burden.

The spirit of America's rule has not been consonant with the manner of the conquest. Civil government was introduced and in 1907 an assembly established, one house being elective by Filipino suffrage. Schools were established with American teachers, and ten years after the suppression of the revolt 440,000 children were in American public schools. In 1916 the Jones Bill made both houses of the assembly elective, and under President Wilson all administrative bureaus were placed under Filipino direction. From the beginning there has been a curb on the exploitation of the Islands, chiefly through a law limiting to 2,500 acres the area of public land that can be purchased by a corporation or individual, and to 2,500 acres more the amount that can be leased. The tariff law has been so administered as to favor American exporters. American goods enter the Islands duty free, other goods must pay duty; whence it will be understood why more than half of the imports of the Philippines are from the United States. And in the early days the tariff was so manipulated as to throw business into the hands of large American corporations. Nevertheless, by comparison with exploitation in territorial possessions elsewhere there has been singular restraint.

Since 1921, however, there has been a marked retrenchment. Under Governor-General Wood a measure of administrative control was restored and a deliberate effort made to bring the reins back into American hands. The result has been years of unbroken deadlock between the American executive and the Filipino legislature. Economically there are even more telling omens. In this the Golden Age of prosperity, chafings against restrictions are to be expected. Grave warnings have been sounded in Congress against the hindrance to progress interposed by the limitation on alienation of public land, such warnings being combined with outcries against the high prices exacted by the British rubber monopoly and glowing pictures of the possibilities of rubber cultivation in the Philippines. Furthermore, the cry of religious freedom has been heard in the land. The religious freedom of whom? Christians, as in infidel Moslem Turkey? To the contrary, the religious freedom of the 1,000,000 Mohammedan Moros of the south, in danger of persecution by the 9,000,000 Christians of the north. That they may worship Allah in peace they must be withdrawn to the direct protection of the United States, Defender of the Faith, free from political infringements and religious bigotries of the Christian Filipinos. By coincidence the land inhabited by the Moros is that which offers the best prospects for growing rubber. Thus with restrictions on religious freedom would go restrictions on economic freedom. One could own all the land one wanted, bring in all the Chinese labor one wanted, and institute the earthly African paradise President McKinley's Ruler of Nations plainly had in mind.

Unfortunately, it is just at the time of retrenchment of Filipino autonomy that Filipinos are most clamorous in demand for independence, a demand that was not modulated by the feud with General Wood. Thus far it has been voiced pacifically but ever more importunately. There exists already an organization extending throughout the Islands for a kind of extra-official administration to circumvent the American executive. Meanwhile the American government repeats at intervals the promise so oft repeated that the Philippines will be freed at some distant and unspecified time when they are "ready for independence," no criteria of readiness being set down.

Of the Filipinos' capacity for self-government much might be said. Their disparate racial elements are still unfused, their dialects differ in various provinces, the sense of political responsibility of most of the inhabitants is still inchoate. Disquieting evidences were revealed in the few years of autonomy, smacking familiarly of Ohio Republicanism. Much might be said about their fitness for self-government, but why? What does it matter? The Filipinos would seize the government and proclaim themselves independent to-morrow if they had the power. And if and when they have the power they will, whether fit for self-government or not. And were they as politically wise as Solons the American government would not give them their independence now, nor a hundred years from now if American interests were to lose thereby. On the one side are Filipino insurgency and such force as the Filipinos can bring to bear; on the other side rubber and oil and exports under favorable tariffs. The issue will be determined by the relative strength of the two sides. Meanwhile there lie in the Philippine Islands all the makings of an American Ireland.

For the record another incident of the Spanish-American War must be chronicled. In 1899, after years of tripartite strife among Great Britain, Germany and the United States over the Samoan Islands, a division was finally effected whereby Germany got the two larger islands and the United States the island of Tutuila, on which it had long had a naval base. Great Britain was compensated elsewhere. The Samoans were not consulted.

The stakes of the Pacific, however, do not lie in islands. They lie in China. Until recent years America's rôle in China was negative. America was, as Americans are passionately fond of telling Chinese, the friend of China. This friendship lay in abstention from grabbing (although, as I have said, American citizens as business men have all the privileges of other foreigners in China) and in espousal of the Open Door policy. This principle, which enjoined every Power from discriminating against other Powers in its territorial concessions or spheres, or in any way limiting equality of commercial opportunity, is unexceptionable as a principle. It is indeed the only basis on which there can be commercial relations between different countries without struggle for monopolistic possession. The Open Door policy merely said: we have battered down the gates of China; let ingress be free to all on equal terms.

It is a sound principle but it also happens to inure to America's advantage. When the other Powers were winning a foothold in China, America's energies were engaged on its own continent. It wanted no overseas possessions. It was a trading nation, exporting goods. Later it became an investing nation, exporting capital. For its own advantage it needed free access everywhere for goods and capital. But thus were nullified all the advantages which other Powers had sought by their military and diplomatic campaigns for concessions and spheres in China.

Judged objectively, the Open Door policy is unassailable. From China's point of view it offers a certain safeguard. Viewed with British, French, Russian and Japanese eyes it opens the way to American profit. Since domination is as unshakable if fastened with investments as if enforced by troops and juridical sovereignties, the Open Door is no barrier to conquest. From any point of view there is something piquant in the fact that America's devotion to the Open Door is less consecrated where the foothold happens to be American. In the Philippines there is no Open Door.

It is interesting to observe how soon, after America began to face outward, its eyes turned in the direction of China, and how soon dollar diplomacy entered the lists against the old-fashioned diplomacy. First, American financial groups demanded a share in railway concessions. After the Russo-Japanese War the Harriman interests sought to buy into the Manchurian railways and then to neutralize the Manchurian railways under joint international administration, projects happily conceived for America's good but unpleasant in the jaundiced eyes of those who already had won the railroads at great sacrifice, namely, Russia and Japan. Despite the urgings of President Taft and Secretary Knox, the American offers were rejected by what was tantamount to a Russo-Japanese alliance.

Then came the Six-Power Consortium, an arrangement for the pooling of loans to China under international supervision. Since a firm clutch on the arterial center of China's government was implicit in the arrangement, President Wilson refused the support of his government to the American group in the consortium. But the world war saw a distinct change in tone. Still proclaiming the Open Door, the United States stood squarely in the way of Japan's swift and unscrupulous penetrations in China, and gave moral support which encouraged China to withstand Japan's bold rush to overpower it while Europe was at war. Before the war was over America took the lead in the formation of a new international consortium, with monopolistic rights to loans to China and provisions for supervision as before. The Chinese, however, have steadfastly refused to accept the consortium's terms.

Immediately after the war American interests procured agreements to erect wireless stations in China, and to reorganize the wine and tobacco bureau with the proceeds of a loan secured on the wine and tobacco tax. The latter plan has never been consummated. American exports to China have increased from $25,000,000 in 1914 to $125,000,000 in 1924, and the number of American firms doing business in China has increased correspondingly.

The disturbances consequent upon internal dissensions and China's defiance of foreign powers have suspended serious American penetration since the war. In the situation created by China's defiance America stands out, with Great Britain, as the leading protagonist of foreign rights, and without America's consent Great Britain has felt unwilling or unable to take disciplinary action. For America is a power in the Far East now, disputing leadership with Great Britain, Russia and Japan. Since all future effort to control China will be by way of finance, the larger pieces in the game are all America's. But the insurgence of Chinese nationalism leaves the nature of the game in doubt for the present. There may even be no game.

The main theatre of American imperial action will be the Pacific, but the stage on which there has been most movement so far is to the south—Central America and the Caribbean. In that direction may be found backward peoples, resources, opportunities for development and investment and political instability, all conditions which beckon to empire. And they beckon only to the United States. By the Monroe Doctrine all other empires are barred out, while by a happy attenuation of it the United States is actually invited in. From the fact that the United States at the close of 1926 had an estimated investment of $4,800,000,000 in Mexico, Cuba, South America and Central America, it may be seen that the interest of the United States is more than platonic; so much more that the Caribbean is now in effect an inland lake of the United States.

The Spanish-American War was fought for the liberation of Cuba from Spanish tyranny, and three years after the war Cuba was given Pickwickian independence. It was proclaimed a sovereign state. But by the Platt Amendment to the Act of Congress conferring sovereignty, Cuba was bound to let the United States have naval bases, to make no treaties and incur no debts of which the United States disapproved, and to submit to intervention by the United States whenever the United States deems that conditions so warrant. Independence!

The right to intervene was exercised in 1906 and threatened in 1912, and the stationing of General E. H. Crowder, of the United States Army, in Cuba since 1919 as high commissioner and ambassador was tantamount to making substantive the informal protectorate. Economically Cuba is not a protectorate but an appendage of the United States. First, by a treaty following on the grant of independence, Cuban sugar was admitted into the United States at a reduction of twenty per cent on the regular duty, while American goods were admitted into Cuba at a corresponding reduction. This has meant, of course, an American monopoly of Cuba's foreign trade. Sugar and tobacco, Cuba's chief crops, are controlled almost completely by the United States, and Cuba takes payment in the form of American manufactured products. It is no accident that out of a total Cuban foreign trade which may be put at a rough average of $685,000,000 a year the share of the United States runs about $550,000,000, or seventy per cent. The American investment in Cuba is estimated at $1,250,000,000, from which it may be rightly inferred that there is very little of value in Cuba not owned by North Americans. So much for liberation. But it must be added that in 1927 Cuba formally asked the United States government to relax the bonds of liberation. It wants a revision of the Platt Amendment.

Porto Rico, also an insular possession of the United States washed by the Caribbean, was annexed by the United States outright, yet its condition does not differ materially from Cuba's except in labels. The executive is appointed by the United States, as are the administrative heads, but the Porto Ricans, who now enjoy the status of American citizens, have a voice in their legislature. Porto Rico being a possession of the United States, the Open Door policy is not applicable. Porto Rican products are admitted into the United States without duty, as are American goods into Porto Rico, whereas imports to Porto Rico from other countries are subject to tariff duty. Hence out of $89,000,000 worth of imports in 1924, $80,000,000 were from the United States; of $87,000,000 worth of exports, $80,000,000 were to the United States.

In both Cuba and Porto Rico, however, sanitation has been introduced, disease is being combated, roads have been built, and peace is maintained.

The story of the Panama Canal is too well known to need detailed rehearsing. The French had had a concession to build a canal across Panama since 1878, but the De Lesseps Company had come to grief in a notorious scandal, and the United States bought it out for $40,000,000. Negotiations were then opened with Colombia, of which Panama was a part, for a lease on territory across the isthmus for $10,000,000 down and $250,000 a year. A treaty was drafted but the Colombian senate refused to ratify, undoubtedly out of a desire to shake down the boundlessly rich uncle from the north. Curiously enough, there was a revolt in Panama against the Colombian government, and, still more curiously, it was led by a Frenchman, none other than Philippe Bunau-Varilla, the engineer who had conducted the negotiations between the United States and the French company, and who was in close touch with the government in Washington. There is documentary evidence that the United States government had indicated that it would look upon such a revolution as a happy event.

Be that as it may, the United States recognized the newly formed Panaman government within three days, and landed Marines to preserve law and order by preventing the approach of Colombian troops to attack the rebels, although Colombia was sovereign over the territory. Negotiations for a lease on what was to be the canal zone now proceeded smoothly, under the eyes of United States Marines, and a few weeks later, in November, 1903, a treaty was signed giving the United States a strip of land ten miles wide for $10,000,000 down and $250,000 a year. In 1927 Panama was pressed to accept another treaty vesting substantial control of its foreign relations in Washington. The Panama affair has always disseminated an unfragrant aroma in American nostrils, and one of President Wilson's first acts was to ask the Senate to authorize payment of $25,000,000 to Colombia by way of damages for the Panama revolution. The Senate refused, but later under a Republican administration consented. There are cynics who say consent followed the discovery of oil in Colombia. They are doubtlessly unjust.

We come now to the more interesting events centering in the island republics of Haiti and Santo Domingo. The Dominican republic, in the way of such principalities when led into temptation, had got itself hopelessly into debt to European powers and the creditors were clamorously demanding payment. To forestall European intervention President Roosevelt intervened himself in 1905, and Santo Domingo consented to America's taking over its customs and supervising its finances. America still does both. In 1916 there broke out one of the insurrections endemic in the Caribbean, and the United States speedily landed Marines to restore order. They remained until 1924.

A new president having been elected in 1916 following the insurrection, the United States offered to recognize his government provided he sign a treaty. Marines being present, recognition was more than legal formality. The United States would obtain by the treaty control of Dominican finances, the army and the civil government, and prior right to the development of resources. Since this meant the end of Dominican independence the new president refused, whereupon the Marines took over the government, dissolved the national assembly, drove civil officials from their desks, and established an absolute military dictatorship. The government of Santo Domingo was thenceforth exercised by officers of the Marines; a censorship was established, protest was punished relentlessly, and a super-czarist régime enforced. In 1924 the Marines were finally withdrawn, but not until a treaty was concluded confirming

American financial receivership. In the interval American finance had bought up everything in the republic, and Santo Domingo is now a subsidiary enterprise of the National City Bank of New York.

Haiti suffered from the example of its neighbor republic. The United States in 1915 had asked the Haitian government to sign a treaty permitting it to administer the Haitian customs and treasury. Haiti refused. In time there was chaos. A revolution broke out, with wholesale massacres and the customary accompaniments. The United States landed Marines, Admiral Caperton in command assuring the Haitian people their integrity would be respected. The Marines are there yet. The request for the right to collect the Haitian customs was renewed, with some embellishments. Haiti was requested also to allow the United States to administer its government, help develop its resources, and intervene when intervention was necessary in American eyes.

The Haitian congress met and elected a president agreeable to the United States, but on being presented with the treaty embodying American wishes it mutinied. Thereupon Admiral Caperton, who held the treasury, refused to pay the members of the congress their salaries and the congress capitulated. A new congress was elected in 1917, and on assembling was given for passage a new constitution drafted in Washington. Among other things the new constitution rescinded the century-old prohibition of land ownership by foreigners. This congress also mutinied, and by way of punition it was summarily dissolved by the Marines. There has never been a Haitian congress since.

The new constitution did not fail of passage, despite the absence of a congress. True to their democratic tradition and practice, the American forces appealed to the people. There was a plebiscite. The Marines watched over the polling places and voting was by open ballot. The people overruled their congress. The constitution was adopted—98,294 for, 789 against. Democracy was vindicated.

The government of Haiti consists of a president, cabinet, and council of state. The council of state elects the president, the president appoints the council of state, the council of state elects the president—agreeable and efficient. But neither president nor council of state can fix the fee for dog licenses without the approval, obtained in advance, of the General commanding the United States Marines. Should the fee displease a Haitian editor and evoke comment in his newspaper, he will be clapped into jail by the United States Marines.

In the interval the National Bank of Haiti has become a branch of the National City Bank of New York, which owns the National Railroad as well. Sugar plantations, smaller railways, public utilities, and nearly everything else are owned in New York. Roads have been built, order maintained (except where American wishes are crossed), sanitation improved, hospitals opened, and an effort made to stamp out the many prevalent diseases.

Let us turn now to Central America—to Nicaragua first. The history of our more intimate relations with Nicaragua opens in 1909, when Nicaragua was under the dictatorship of President Zelaya, whose unconstitutional practices disturbed the United States very little until he showed favoritism to Europeans in his loan policy and lukewarmness toward American ambitions for a naval base. In the natural course of events a revolution broke out. It is not certain whether this was endemic or inoculated. But it seems clear that the United States knew it was coming, and that it was led by gentlemen not prejudiced against the United States. Among the rebels were two American filibusters who were captured and executed, properly according to the rules of war, but Secretary of State Knox was shocked and broke off diplomatic relations. In brief, the revolution was successful, Zelaya resigned, and José Madriz was lawfully elected to succeed him, although the leaders of the revolution were Juan Estrada, General Chamorro, and one Adolfo Diaz, an employe of an American mining company at $1,000 a year who had managed to save $600,000 out of his salary to finance a revolution. His name should be marked. It figures prominently in these chronicles.

Unfortunately Madriz indicated that his first loyalty would be to Nicaragua, and the Estrada-Chamorro-Diaz revolution was resumed, with arms and ammunition shipped from the United States. When it appeared that Madriz was about to crush the rebels, United States Marines were landed and the Madriz forces kept at a distance. Madriz was of course defeated. In the meantime the rebel leaders concluded with an American representative on board an American warship the so-called Dawson Pact, whereby Estrada was to be president, with Diaz in reserve, and Nicaragua was to contract a loan from the United States.

Estrada became president in due course, but the Dawson Pact aroused a storm in Nicaragua when it became known, and the assembly proceeded to adopt a constitution forbidding foreign control through loans. The assembly was dissolved for its refractoriness, but the business was a little too much for Estrada. In 1911 he resigned in favor of the thrifty Señor Diaz, who is president again now in 1927. Señor Diaz being less stiff-necked, there followed a bewildering succession of treaties and loan agreements putting the Nicaraguan customs, the National Bank of Nicaragua, the railroads of Nicaragua, and a good deal else in Nicaragua under American control. The United States Senate refused to ratify the most glaring of the treaties, so it was put into effect piecemeal and indirectly.

The treaties were glaring to the Nicaraguan

people as well, and there was a revolt against Diaz. United States Marines were landed opportunely and the revolt was crushed. Diaz remained in office until 1916, and the Marines in Nicaragua until 1925. In 1916 the pacifistic Secretary of State Bryan negotiated the Bryan-Chamorro treaty, whereby for $3,000,000, to be expended as the United States directed, the United States got the right to construct a canal across Nicaragua whenever it wished, and leases on the Corn Islands and a naval base on the Gulf of Fonseca, any one of which would have been cheap at the price. In 1918 a high commission, with two American members out of three, was empowered to supervise Nicaraguan finances.

In 1925 the United States Marines were withdrawn. There was held soon after an election in which Carlos Solorzano was elected president and Juan Sacasa vice-president. General Chamorro, the defeated candidate, started a revolt. Solorzano then resigned and by law Sacasa should have succeeded him, but Chamorro had military backing and was elected by a packed assembly. It was hardly constitutional, and the Department of State, faithful to democratic procedure, persuaded Chamorro to resign. There was another election by the packed assembly, and it chose none other than the thrifty Diaz under whom there had been such amicable relations with the United States. To the refractory Nicaraguans this again seemed thick, and when

Sacasa called for support for his cause they rallied to him. When it appeared once more that Diaz was to be booted out, the United States Marines returned, in 1926, and with their aid Diaz was victorious. The Marines have had to stay, not only to protect Mr. Diaz in his capital but to police the country.

Law and order being restored, Mr. Coolidge's government sent an unofficial representative to Nicaragua to lay the basis of a lasting peace. He persuaded the rebels to lay down their arms with the telling argument that the United States would kill them if they did not. Loving life, they did. In return the United States promised to supervise the next elections. Is one presumptuous in assuming that the suffrage will eventuate in the reëlection of the good Diaz or someone who shares his predilections, and that the United States Marines will be landed whenever that gentleman's tenure is threatened by refractory Nicaraguans? Is one presumptuous also in closing the story of Nicaragua by classifying it as one with Haiti and Santo Domingo and Porto Rico?

Elsewhere in Central America the progress of events has been less dramatic, but undramatically the same process has been going forward. Economic and financial control is being vested in New York. Banks, railroads, mines, public utilities and plantations are being bought up by North American banks and syndicates. In time there will be chaos, American lives and property will be endangered, and Marines will be landed. The fact is worth observation and remembrance that, notorious as are political instability and economic insecurity in Central America, the investments of the United States in Central America have increased enormously in ten years. There has been a veritable rush of capital into the five Central American countries. So far from being frightened by the certainties of revolutions and disorder, American capital seems to welcome the prospect. No doubt the oft-demonstrated willingness of the American government to neutralize the terrors of the prospect heartens American investors to face it. No doubt they go in order to be protected by the government when chaos comes, or even hoping that they will be in need of protection. But much light is thrown thus on the respectable and official contention that it is the inability of such countries as the Central American republics to govern themselves that creates situations in which strong and efficient countries are reluctantly forced to intervene.

We come finally to Mexico. Relations with Mexico have been more complicated but less exigent than with its neighboring republics. First, Mexico was governed for thirty years by the dictator Porfirio Diaz, who while dictatorial to the Mexicans was benevolent to foreign investors. British and American oil operators, mine owners and landowners were unimpeded by him in their efforts for the common good. There was no occasion for solicitude on the part of Washington. Second, Mexico has a population of nearly 15,000,000, and an area in which a small expeditionary force of Marines would be lost.

In 1911 Diaz, whose firmness of grasp was relaxing with age, was overthrown by Madero and all the submerged discontent of a generation was loosed at once. The festering sores in the social body, salved over for years, were torn open and released malignant poisons, as is always the way after dictatorships. The Madero revolution was only the first of a series, and it may be that the series is but scarcely begun. Revolutions in Mexico are more than insurrecto amusements and Latin-American political effervescence. They spring from grave social maladjustments, especially in distribution of land. The Mexican peon, disinherited for generations, is asserting himself. Until the agrarian and labor problems can be solved Mexico cannot regain equilibrium, and foreign enterprise will be prosecuted under difficulties.

To the United States in particular this fact is of more than doctrinal import. Under Diaz American interests flourished. American citizens now have more than a billion dollars invested in Mexico; by some the figure is put as high as a billion and a quarter. The largest share of this is in oil, between $500,000,000 and $750,000,000, and the rest is in mines, agricultural lands and railroads. When the Department of State affirms the necessity of protecting property in Mexico it deals in no metaphors.

Of the successive Mexican revolutions since 1911 it is unnecessary to speak here. For our purpose their significance is that through them the United States has come to play a more and more direct part in determining the fate of Mexican governments, by granting or withholding recognition and by the use of the embargo on arms. By refusing to recognize Huerta President Wilson doomed him to downfall. By the arms embargo the United States can make revolutions in Mexico or frustrate them. Twice since 1911 the United States has actually intervened in Mexico by force of arms: in 1914 over a ceremonial dispute, and in 1916 after the bandit leader Villa had made raids over the American border. Little need be said concerning the grave charges of meddling in Mexican politics made against foreign oil interests. British and American oil syndicates have been flatly accused of underwriting Mexican revolutions in order to put into power factions favorable to themselves. There is no authentic evidence definitively to confirm such charges, but that highly organized and heavily endowed propaganda campaigns have been conducted in the United States to convert American opinion to "cleaning up" Mexico is too obvious for comment.

The real point of issue between the United States and Mexico, that which has brought the two to deadlock, is economic—primarily oil. Mexico's revolution is social no less than political. It is aimed at restoring Mexico's wealth to Mexico, and giving all classes of Mexicans an opportunity to win a fair share. To that end there was embodied in the Mexican Constitution of 1917 the famous Article 27, vesting in the nation ownership of all sub-soil products and in effect nationalizing land. By the enabling acts passed to carry out Article 27 it is provided that no foreigner may acquire land within a hundred kilometers of the land frontiers or fifty kilometers of the coasts. Foreigners who now hold such lands may retain them until their death, after which the lands must be sold. Corporations must dispose of such land within ten years. With regard to petroleum products it is provided that while sub-soil products are the property of the nation the government may grant concessions for their exploitation; but that all owners of oil lands and concessions shall register their titles with the government for confirmation, and obtain in return concessions for fifty years with an optional renewal for thirty years thereafter. Furthermore, all foreign owners of land and mineral or oil concessions are Mexican nationals in respect to their properties, and bind themselves not to invoke the support of their own governments in any dispute with Mexico. In other words, foreigners own property in Mexico on the same basis as Mexicans.

The American government's position, in support of American oil operators and landowners, is that the

Mexican oil and land laws are retroactive, since they cover rights obtained before the adoption of the Constitution of 1917, and that they are confiscatory. The Mexican government's position is that they are not retroactive, and it points to the specific injunction in the constitution against retroactive application. It maintains that compulsory registration of concessions obtained before 1917 is not retroactive, since all legitimate titles will be confirmed.

Up to the present time most of the American oil interests have refused to register their titles. The issue is before the Mexican courts for adjudication. Should the courts uphold the oil laws the Mexican government will be empowered to declare void the concessions of foreigners who refuse to register and will confiscate their property. In that case the United States must either support its nationals or retreat from the position it has taken. The sum involved being not much less than a billion dollars, and those who stand to lose the billion being highly influential personages, doubt may be entertained whether the American government will retreat. If it does not . . . perhaps destiny has so planned from the beginning.

If and when it comes to the fulfillment of destiny, whatever be the immediate and provoking cause, whether confiscation of American property, or killing of twenty American citizens, or, as is more likely, law and order and legality and the sanctity of private property and national honor and civilization and humanity—the real, underlying cause will be investments and profits. The fundamental issue will be whether a country, though militarily weak, can solve its domestic social problems by measures which inflict loss on citizens of another country, though militarily strong. Practically, the fundamental issue is this: Can any Latin-American country take any measures, even for its own social good, that hurt North American property rights?

On the American continent, in conclusion, we see all the elements which when fused produce the compound of imperialism. They are being fused now. What has been elsewhere is now here. As with the strong states of Europe, so with the United States of America. To anyone with a sense of history the portents are unmistakable. The United States is on the march. It is out of no neurasthenic morbidity that all Latin America from the Rio Grande to the Horn is united in one sentiment, a sentiment mixed equally of fear and hatred of the Colossus of the North whose shadow already is thrown before.

The United States is among the empires. A book on imperialism in 1927 might very well begin with the recent history of the United States.

CHAPTER XIV

THE RECKONING

WHEN Chinese nationalism began to take the form of a direct anti-foreign movement in 1926 and the British Concession in Hankow was attacked, a demand for immediate military intervention was voiced by one faction in England. Its spokesman was Lord Birkenhead, Secretary of State for India. Now that the Chinese were openly attacking foreigners and foreign interests, he said, the Powers must take drastic action, regardless of the value of the interests affected. Something greater was at stake—their prestige. Uprisings anywhere must be repressed at once or the prestige of the white man would be lost everywhere. The subject nationalities would challenge their rulers with impunity, and the position of the Western Powers would become untenable throughout the East. China's insubordination must not be allowed to go unpunished lest it be construed as a signal for a general mutiny. Disciplinary measures must be taken at once, if only for didactic effect.

It was harsh doctrine, enunciated with brutal frankness, and it provoked an outcry of protest from British and American liberals. Yet it stated an incontrovertible truth. Its only weakness lay in that it was voiced too late. White prestige had already been lost beyond recovery. Moral prestige had been dimmed for reasons I have analyzed in some detail. There remained only the prestige of power, the ability to bring up armaments to punish rebellion or disobedience. And this had been seriously impaired by the war.

To any Asiatic at all familiar with contemporary affairs it was apparent that both sides had been spent by the war, that their governments would for years lack the resources to prosecute another war, and that their people would have no stomach for war, least of all a war on a distant nation of which they scarcely had heard. The only Western Power which could muster effective force was the United States, but it was least inclined to do so, except in the Philippines, where disaffection was not yet in a critical stage. If confirmation were needed, it was afforded by Turkey. I have already told how Turkey successfully defied the Allied Powers, and how the British government had to swallow its chagrin because the British public, especially in the Dominions, turned a deaf ear to Mr. Lloyd George's impassioned appeal to stand in the breaches for Christianity. No sophisticated man in the East needed to be told that if Great Britain took its hands off the long-coveted prize of Constantinople it did so because there was no alternative. China offered further evidence.

THE WHITE MAN'S DILEMMA

The Chinese had lost their supplicant airs. They no longer walked in humility as of old. They had become unsubmissive. Not only were demands made for abrogation of foreign treaties infringing China's sovereignty, but foreign treaties were violated and foreign citizens roughly handled. In 1925 a local strike in Shanghai flared up into a general strike against foreigners, a boycott of foreign trade and attacks on foreign residents. Not since Boxer days had the Chinese permitted themselves such liberties. Soon after, there was a skirmish on the Yangtsze River in which Chinese fired on and killed British subjects on a British warship. Twenty-five years before a similar incident would have resulted in occupation of half a dozen Chinese ports, a huge indemnity, resignation of Chinese cabinet ministers, and a few railway and mining concessions. This time the British contented themselves with bombarding one town and killing a few thousand Chinese. They did not even make a "diplomatic incident" out of the affair. The inference, all too plain, was drawn by any Chinese. The British could do nothing else. They could not now send an expedition big enough to impose penalties on the old scale. So it has been with all of China's numerous offenses in recent years. The Western Powers make "formal diplomatic protests." They do nothing. The inference becomes a conclusion; and Indians, among others, take note.

Hence Lord Birkenhead's very proper concern and irrefutable analysis.

White prestige had passed before Lord Birkenhead spoke. The old symbol had lost its value. The days were gone when one regiment could keep a whole countryside docile because the regiment represented something distant but invincible and terrible, a force that could be summoned to deal destruction. Our power was now to be taken only on its face value. It had to be demonstrated. Unfortunately the demonstration was not very impressive. For those who had feared it, now if ever was the time to put it to the test.

The Birkenheads saw this clearly. To all men in the Colonial Offices of empires with Asiatic possessions it has long been an axiom that the native can be held in check only by force. Any concession made by the ruling empire is interpreted by the Oriental as a sign of weakness and he immediately demands more. With this axiom to guide them, the officials of Western empires in Eastern dependencies—the British especially, for they have had the widest experience in imperial administration—have usually been uncompromising beyond the immediate necessities of the situation. They have "kept the native in his place" politically just to show they could. Every conciliatory measure, every grant of minor rights in the direction of self-government proposed by the authorities at home, has been opposed by the "men on the spot" with the full weight of their influence and authority, and accepted by them only under compulsion from home and then with fatalistic forewarnings. When General Dyer at Amritsar opened fire on the demonstrating Punjabi masses, shot down some two thousand and forced the others to crawl on hands and knees, he was acting in conformance with every tenet of the philosophy his career had instilled in him. Every British-Indian Army officer would avoid such extremities if possible, but if not he would resort to the same measures out of the same philosophy.

It is an ugly philosophy, the philosophy of the jungle. But it is absolutely unassailable. And every detached individual who knows the East, however much his own instincts may rebel, must admit that it is deduced from actual phenomena accurately observed. Given the premise that one nation may rule another because stronger and more efficient, any rule of action not based on this philosophy is a mistake and in contravention of the premise. Given the premise—but only if the premise be given—the Kitcheners, Curzons, General Woods, General Dyers and Japanese commanders in Korea are unanswerable. The native does interpret concession or conciliation as a sign of weakness, as an indication that if he presses the advantage he will get more. He immediately demands more, and if he gets it demands still more, until, as the officers in the colonies say, "Where will it all end?" And the unspoken conclusion that it ends in the natives' driving their rulers out is indisputable. The only preventive, therefore, is to hold the reins tight, make no concessions, not even such as are intrinsically safe, suffer not the slightest diminution in mastery. From the point of view of practical politics imperialism admits of no compromise.

Unfortunately the nineteenth century was a time of humanitarian liberalism, side by side with if not combined with practical international politics. The humanitarian liberals were articulate and vocal and, to the discomfort of the practical, were men of character and qualities which commanded general respect. Their words carried weight among the populace and had to be heeded, if only in outward form. Moreover, since our professions of motive for imperialistic aggression were all high-minded, it was awkward to make open answer to the liberals with the only argument that was effective, that is, the argument drawn from the philosophy of the jungle. So concessions were made, though usually coincidental with the appeals of the liberals rather than because of them. Natives were allowed to elect a few members of their legislatures, to hold minor posts in administrative bureaus, and to voice their opinions in vernacular papers if the opinions were not too outspoken and disrespectful.

These concessions were a mistake. The liberals were shortsighted. As usual, they wanted to eat their cake and have it; they were unwilling to forego the advantages inhering in access to the riches of the dependencies, and unwilling to pay the price in ugliness exacted for the riches of the dependencies. Even to-day most of them say we cannot give up India or the Philippines, we must be guided by altruism. But whether the measures of conciliation are attributable to the urgings of liberals or to other factors, they have been a mistake. All the ominous forebodings of the most reactionary colonial army officers have been vindicated. For the colonial administrator the task has been made immeasurably harder, perhaps impossible. Every palliative measure, every conciliatory grant has planted the seed of intransigence. The crop is the demand for independence now heard on every side.

In order to sweeten the pill for millions of old-fashioned Americans who gagged at their first imperialistic dose, the American government sent teachers to the Philippines, taught the Filipinos to read and write even in the remote interior, gave them a legislature and then, in 1916, autonomy and a promise of independence. The present widespread insurgency is the result. We should have governed with proconsuls and unrelenting firmness, as the Spanish did but without the provocative Spanish cruelties. And if the writer were to be summoned by

President Coolidge and offered the post of governor-general of the Philippine Islands with instructions so to act as to relieve the present tension he would accept on one condition only, the condition that he could go out to Manila and within ninety days do one of two things: appoint American bureaucrats to every post, clap a Czarist censorship on the Islands, forbid freedom of speech, and take Quezon, Osmena, Roxas and other Independencista leaders, put them against a wall and shoot them—or else run down the American flag and clear out the American occupation, root and branch. Somebody else would be appointed.

The axiom of the colonial bureaucrat is based on accurate observation; so is the axiom of the native that whatever he gets is given only because he is strong enough to exact it and that he may as well get as much as possible while in that relative position. He, too, is generalizing only from experience. Since European Powers began to rule Eastern territories they have never, as a matter of fact, made any concessions unless they had to, unless disaffection was running so high as to threaten revolution. No grant of rights to dependent peoples has ever been given spontaneously. The exception of the United States, which was an amateur in imperialism, and was moreover constrained to its original liberalism in the Philippines by domestic politics, merely validates the rule. Self-government for the Boers after the Boer

War may be explained by the fact that Campbell-Bannerman, the British Premier, was unique in politics; even so, it followed, it did not precede the war. The generalization holds. Even Canada was not allowed responsible self-government until after the rebellion of 1837. Not until after the Sepoy Rebellion of 1857 was the East India Company divested of its power in India, and direct responsibility lodged in the British civil government with a Secretary of State accountable to Parliament. Only after the education of large numbers of Indians in English universities had instilled in them ideas of nationalism and democracy and stirred up sentiments which had become vocal, were Indian representatives named to the Council of the Secretary of State for India and the Council of the Viceroy. And only after Mr. Montagu, in the report already quoted, had found the discontent which later culminated in the Gandhi movement, were the Montagu-Chelmsford reforms instituted by which Indians have at least the echo of a voice in their government. The system of the dyarchy allows the elective provincial councils to exercise the right of decision in matters of lesser importance, while control of the army, police courts and finance are reserved, as it is put, to the British executive.

The most conspicuous illustration is the recent course of events in China. For years China had come before the Powers as a supplicant for small favors, asking that the Powers relinquish only a few of their privileges. China asked permission to raise its tariff above the five per cent level and the beginning of modification of the status of extraterritoriality. The first formal request was made at the Paris Peace Conference, when reconstruction was being ushered in. Receipt was acknowledged and the petition pigeonholed. The next request was made at the Washington Conference in 1921 in a little greater detail. For answer China was treated to a homily on the need of learning to govern itself honestly and efficiently—this, mind, in the Washington of the Harding administration where subsequently the very paving-stones were to be unsafe. By way of consolation, however, the Powers there assembled did agree to remove their own post offices from Chinese soil, to hold a conference to draw up a new tariff schedule for China, and to "investigate" the situation with regard to extraterritoriality.

The Chinese delegates went home disgruntled and there found opinion still more disgruntled. Then came the strike of 1925. The Chinese arose in wrath and expressed themselves with violence. When the foreign Powers made their customary threats the Chinese answered with derisive remarks. And within six weeks the treaties signed at the Washington Conference, which had remained a dead letter because France refused to ratify, were suddenly ratified and the Powers set themselves busily to conferring over the tariff. Again the Chinese drew inferences. They violated the foreign treaties, beat up foreigners, killed foreigners. Finally they attacked the British Concession. For answer Mr. Austen Chamberlain, the British Foreign Minister, sent to the other Powers his famous note declaring that a new policy of conciliation must be adopted to China, that a new spirit must inform our attitude toward China, and that we must meet the legitimate aspirations of the Chinese nation. The Chinese position, he said, might be in contravention of the treaties, but "this does not sufficiently take into account the realities of the situation."

So: When the Chinese made their appeals on grounds of reason and justice, they were met with polite scorn and indifference. But when they arose and began smiting about them, showing that they cared little for the right or wrong but intended to take what they could get by their own efforts, by fighting if they had to, then suddenly we became aware of right and wrong, suddenly the way of morality was made plain to us. Then we proposed renunciation of "a policy . . . capable of being regarded as an encroachment on . . . the sovereignty and independence of China." And Mr. Secretary Kellogg of the American Cabinet spoke in similar vein, though simultaneously ordering more and more Marines to Nicaragua to encroach on the sovereignty and independence of Nicaragua, which has a very small population and a very weak army. Why the sudden revelation of morality? Why were China's appeals so much more cogent than when based on reason and pacifically submitted? Because they were backed by force, because China had acted unpleasantly.

Whatever may be true of their relations among themselves, the white nations in their relations with peoples they consider inferior have so acted as to instill the belief that they respect only one quality—force. And I believe it can be substantiated that in their relations with other peoples the white nations do respect that one quality alone. I have told how foreigners conduct themselves nearly everywhere in the East. I have told how in a Chinese port they kick elderly men off the street, slap clerks, beat up their servants. Nerves; the pressure of an alien environment, irritating habits, differences of custom. But I have seen the same men in Japan, two days' sailing away. How quickly they control themselves there! They do not boot an aged Japanese out of the way. Why? If they did, a crowd would gather and break their heads unless the police came to the rescue and took them into safe custody.

So also in the realms of international relations. Whatever the Powers may have done or attempted, they have never dared to go so far in Turkey as elsewhere in the East. Until a hundred and fifty years ago they fought Turkey as a respected enemy.

Only since Turkey began to lose military strength has Europe adopted a bullying policy. Even then one has not read of foreign fleets shelling Turkish ports, landing troops and holding cities until treaties are signed granting settlements and concessions to fabulously rich mining regions because one foreigner was accidentally killed by brigands. Only in the last few years the nationalistic régime of Mustapha Kemal has dealt cavalierly with American mission colleges and Y. M. C. A. branches, still more cavalierly with British business houses. Has the Turk been "disciplined?" And why not? Because the Turk can fight. Every European foreign office knows that if it stretch too rapacious a hand over Turkey, regiments of Anatolian peasants will snap it off. By contemplation of the danger Europe has learned that justice is due an Oriental country if in the Near East, not the Far East. And the native infidel Turk sits in the lounge of the Constantinople Club with a fez on his head. For the same reason.

One marked contrast between the Near East and Far East impresses itself on one who knows both. This is the comparative religious liberalism and religious tolerance of the missionary in the Near East. The American missionary in Turkey does not cry "Heathen"—aloud. He does not force proselyting on those who are unwilling. He does not proselyte at all among the Moslems. He is even broad-minded about the abstract right to proselyte. Not only does he not voice his bigotry, he has been broadened out of bigotry. No Turkish mosque is invaded by a foreigner shouting to men bent in prayer to turn from the vain worship of idols and give ear unto the truth. But Far Eastern temples are. It is an interesting commentary that among a gentle, passive, religiously tolerant people like the Chinese, missionaries are arrogant, aggressive, insensitive to the natives' religious feelings and bigoted; among an aggressive, combative, fierce, religiously intolerant people like the Turks they are considerate, tactful, religiously liberal and not insistent on the propagation of their own religious beliefs. Why? They are of the same class as those I have described elsewhere in the East. Why? Because the Turk is sensitive about his religion, like all Moslems, and will impale on the bayonet those who insult his faith. It is the broadening influence of force that has taught the missionary tolerance, as it has taught the business man courtesy even toward a native, and his government restraint even toward an oriental state.

In the mind of all educated men of other races there is a firmly rooted conviction that the white man in the mass responds to one form of appeal only, the club and a stout arm to swing it. Hold the club ready and show that you can swing it to effect, and the white man will see the claims of justice and deal justly; and only then. It is a conviction supported by history. Further and more to the point, the conviction is now being acted upon. Our dependencies, it is true, cannot be held in check except by force. They attribute any tender of conciliation as evidence of fear. But also they have learned that only force on their part will gain them any amelioration of their condition, even such as is warranted in justice. None can say where the circle begins, and it does not matter. When the preponderance of force was ours, we could be humanitarian if we liked or Czarist if we liked. Those we ruled had to submit and did. Now the preponderance of force is in doubt. The doubt is strong enough for those we rule to put it to the test, for now by their formula is the appointed time, now the time to harvest the crop of long-growing aspirations and long-planted hates.

With the exception of Belgium and Italy, whose imperial possessions are in the primitive stage or, like Tripoli, are bound helpless, there is not an empire which has not had a mutinous subject nationality on its hands since the war. Excepting those which are primitive, as in inner Africa, or bound helpless, there is not a subject nationality which is not openly or covertly mutinous. Those which felt themselves strong enough have been openly so, and these include the possessions which are most valuable. The critical stage of imperialism, the last stage of the cycle in which we return to the first and have to establish conquest over our possessions, has just begun.

Turkey revolted successfully and won back the

sovereignty it had lost in the world war. Egypt, with a sense of betrayal after the war, gained impetus for the nationalism which had been growing since the British occupation. Before the Paris Peace Conference closed riots had broken out in Cairo, the British had to rush reinforcements to their garrisons, and Zaghlul Pasha, the nationalist leader, was deported. Thus the flame was fanned higher and Zaghlul was allowed to return. There were renewed riots, again he was deported. So serious was the situation that the British sent a commission to investigate, and on its recommendation was adopted the plan of quasi-independence already outlined. Zaghlul was permitted to return once more and was made premier. Trouble broke out again in 1925 when Sir Lee Stack, governor-general of the Sudan, was assassinated. Then the British applied their disciplinary measures and the nationalists were crushed. But Egypt was left seething, and in the summer of 1927 British warships had to be sent again, since the Egyptians were demanding removal of the British commander of their army. For though Egypt is officially independent, the British advisers, the term euphemistically applied to them, remain in strategic positions. Egypt seethes and will run over again.

The Riffian tribes in Morocco overwhelmed Spain and compelled France to fight a two years' war before Abd el-Krim, the leader of the Riffi, surrendered. In South Africa there is not so much the conventional imperialistic situation as smouldering race resentment on the part of blacks, half-castes and Hindus for whom an economic as well as social pale has been erected. And there are yet unreconstructed Boers, although their position is too complex to be simply classified. Abyssinia has voiced vigorous protest at the League of Nations against proposed encroachments by Great Britain and Italy.

In Syria there was an uprising so menacing the French had to send an expedition and then shell and partly destroy the ancient city of Damascus. The rebellious Druses were crushed and, although a not too thorough investigation by the League of Nations Mandate Commission brought some relief, anti-French feeling smoulders. It will flame again. The Arabs overthrew Hussein, the British-picked king of the Hedjaz, and would do the same in Irak and Trans-Jordania if they dared. In Persia there is a lusty nationalistic movement which has balked British efforts for a formal protectorate and then for a resumption of the old domination, minus the rivalry of imperial Russia. In Java and Sumatra there have been so-called communist uprisings in 1926 and 1927, which have had to be put down by military action. For the first time conscious unrest begins to manifest itself in the Dutch East Indies. The ferment in China proper has spread to French Indo-China and the French have had to take the alert. Of the Philippines I have already spoken.

THE RECKONING

The arena in which the issue will be fought out, however, is China and India. In China the conflict is at critical stage already. The Chinese of every stripe, from the Red fringe to the old mandarinate, are united in demand for retrocession of all privileges granted foreigners. It is not little favors they ask now. They demand complete liquidation of the system built up since 1842, even to reversion of the leaseholds and territorial concessions. The Powers who hold the privileges must yield or fight. The issue appeared to have reached a climax early in 1927, when British and American armed forces had to be sent in large numbers. It subsided, owing to internal dissensions. It will move forward thus in waves, now on the crest and now subsiding. At some period when it is at the crest there may be another onslaught on foreigners as there was at Nanking in March, 1927, not a few but many foreigners will be killed, and there will be another Boxer war, with the difference that in 1900 only the fanatic Boxer society was involved while now the whole Chinese people will be engaged; there are 400,000,000. Either that or the Powers must seize the advantage of a period of subsidence, and by peaceful negotiations set up a new basis of relations with China, beginning with a complete revision of the treaties. Promises in generalities and trivial relinquishments will no longer suffice as they would have sufficed ten years ago. We would not make them then. We

THE WHITE MAN'S DILEMMA

did not have to. Nor do we show any more indication of willingness now to consider making even minor relinquishments in such periods of subsidence as have followed the turbulent events of March, 1927. Only when confronted by violence do we show inclination to be reasonable, and then reasonableness is futile. But whether by the arbitrament of war or by peaceful negotiation, the Chinese question must be settled in the immediate future. And since settlement has been delayed so long, the only terms possible are virtual surrender by the Occident. The alternative is war on the scale of world calamity, for a continent cannot be policed by a few regiments of Marines, and a quarter of the human race subdued by a corps. War on a scale of a million troops, extended over years, is the alternative. Repressive measures taken swiftly and relentlessly a few years ago when nationalism first became clamant might have averted the necessity of choice between extremes. Or, the offer of alleviations might have done so. Either course would have been logical, consistent and perhaps effective. We did neither. We did not send expeditions to shell nationalist centers and capture and execute nationalist leaders, which might have crushed the movement for some years and which would have been easier before the movement was full-blown. Nor, on the other hand, did we attempt to placate nationalistic sentiment. Now it is too late for any measures except the extremes. Empires are always too late. That appears to be inherent in the institution.

In India the imprisonment of Gandhi broke the spirit of the non-coöperative movement, which for a time menaced the British raj as it had not been menaced since the Mutiny. But non-coöperation, that is, passive resistance and refusal to pay taxes, was too elusive for sustained mass loyalty. Probably passive resistance will always either be galvanized into violence or will diffuse in mere talk. There has been also a recrudescence of hostilities between Hindu and Moslem. India is at the moment quiescent, but that it can be for longer than the moment, none believes who knows India. The ferment has seethed too long. A test will come in 1929, when the Montagu-Chelmsford plan comes up for revision. The British have an opportunity to forestall extremities by liberal grants of privileges in the direction of autonomy. The temper of the present British government, in which Lord Birkenhead is Secretary for India, makes such a prospect dubious. Birkenhead is an advocate of discipline. He may be right. The example of China will fire all India. But if the policy of prestige and discipline is followed, as quite likely it must be, then the issue is drawn beyond possibility of compromise and will be determined by extremities. That the next generation will see Great Britain's task in India immeasurably more arduous is fact, not prophecy, no matter what the outcome may be.

For record this must be said. So much has been made in statesmen's speeches and in the press about Bolshevik incitation of revolt in Asia that cognizance must be taken. The Bolsheviki have indeed spread propaganda in Asia. They always did, for there Great Britain was vulnerable. This propaganda has had some effect, especially in China. It has the same relation to the grave condition in China as a digestive disorder in one suffering from cancer. It is unpleasant, it is a complication, and it may even hasten the end by a very little, but the organic malady, that of which the patient is dying, is cancer. The fevers now shaking the East are the outward signs of the deep-lying, organic disturbances I have tried to diagnose. They would have stricken the East if Nicholas II, his wife and Rasputin were still playing at magic in Tsarskoe-Selo. They were manifesting symptoms when the Bolsheviki were still hemmed in within their own boundaries by counter-revolutions and the Allied *cordon sanitaire*. The crisis would be equally grave now had the Bolsheviki never come out of blockade or had there never been any Bolsheviki.

CHAPTER XV

WHAT MIGHT HAVE BEEN

GIVEN the premise of empire, I have said, the philosophy of force is unimpeachable. If one nation has the right to rule another because stronger and more efficient, then compromise or conciliation is a mistake. Any relaxation in the direction of greater freedom for our subject nationalities prompted by considerations of justice or sympathy only undermines our position. This should be amplified. The syllogism more aptly fits the system we are analyzing if it opens: given the premise of empire for the purposes for which we seek empires, given the right to rule other nations for the objects for which we want to rule them. Then the conclusion follows as I have stated it.

There is no fixed law in the nature of the universe that a nation cannot stand in tutelary relation to a weaker nation without such abuses that its position rests on might alone. In the abstract there is no reason why one nation cannot have full power of rulership over another without invoking the arbitrament of force. It is not likely, to be sure, but it has not been demonstrated to be impossible; it is at least conceivable. But then a different spirit must animate both tutelage and tutor.

The Western Powers needed raw materials and markets. The need was compelling, since it grew out of an industrialized society. In certain regions in Asia and Africa were plenteous stores of raw materials and millions of prospective buyers for our finished products. The inhabitants of those regions were incapable of developing their resources. Nor could they learn without instruction and supervision by those already technically competent. We could have exercised supervision, even insisted that we be allowed to exercise it, but with recognition of equality as nations and individuals, while acknowledging disparity in technical proficiency and social efficiency. We could have gone in slowly, seeking first to understand the people, their psychology and their social foundations, and erecting a new scaffolding without displacing the foundations. We could have taken them into partnership and then proceeded to extract their riches.

Since the native people had equal voice and acted by their own consent on being convinced of the wisdom of so doing—convincing them would have been easy, as the appeal of greater wealth is intrinsically cogent—the development of resources and the consequent social changes would have gone forward as the population adjusted itself to the changes without constriction or distortion, instead of being accelerated so as to throw the indigenous society out of balance and produce an unintegrated economy such as exists in India. There would have been a natural, healthy evolution. Simultaneously we could have transmitted the social advantages we derive from scientific progress. Roads could have been built, sanitary systems installed, schools opened, hospitals distributed throughout the country, and better political administration established. As the inhabitants became more proficient in the new technology we could have slowly admitted them into a larger share of executive positions and ourselves slowly receded.

Politically we should have trained young men to hold minor administrative posts, promoting them as they grasped the principles of government according to system and impersonal law. Instead of waiting for subterranean discontent to explode in angry popular demonstrations for self-rule, we should have introduced a native minority into legislative councils, anticipating the demand rather than grudgingly yielding to it. The minority could have been gradually enlarged, progressively with the increase of authority in industry. But, most of all, every such enlargement of the status of the natives would precede not follow demand. It could be granted then without whetting appetites for more. There would be none of the hostility which prompts the desire to get all at once. And thus we should have had to give less than has been the case in fact.

Also, of course, and equally important, the "we" would not have been rival British, French and Germans but an international pooling of efforts and interests with a pro rata division of raw materials, markets and profits. On the one hand we should have not had to contend against two obstructions, native hostility and native technical ignorance, one of which was unnecessary. On the other hand we should not have had British, French and Germans intriguing against each other, checkmating each other and cutting each other's throats. We should not have had to spend our energies in international conflict.

So it might have been. What has been is as we know. The spirit in which the Powers went out into the undeveloped parts of the earth was exclusively the spirit of grab. Our sole object was easy and quick profits, and we disembowelled the earth and instituted a native serfdom and governed as autocratic satraps in order that we might not be interfered with. What happened to the people whose ill-fortune it was to reside in places containing objects of value—whether the alien and exotic growths we thrust into their soil undermined their institutions—to all the consequences of exploitation we were indifferent. Whatever hindrance there was to our amassing profits quickly, whether deliberately interposed or there by virtue of indigenous conditions, we trod down in our stride. We wanted raw materials, all of them; a monopoly on them. Access to raw materials was imperative, the irresistible command of the industrialism to which the West had committed itself. But procuring them in that manner and that spirit was not imperative. It was not a social mandate but a private acquisitive motive. For the social well-being of the Western countries themselves it might have been better had they not been able to industrialize with so violent a rush. There might have been even in England and the United States a healthier ordering of progress. The ghastly factory towns that disfigured and still disfigure what once were settings of quiet beauty would have been spared us. So also the ruthless squandering of natural resources reckless of the future; and, most of all, the destruction of human material in fourteen-hour days and twelve-hour days at wages based on the scale of labor in household and craft production. The horrors of the English factory town in 1820 or the coal mining towns in the United States still later are of the same growth as forced labor in Africa and the duel for concessions in the East. The maladjustments still crippling our society to-day were formed in the anarchic chaos of our own industrialization. It was not a social motive, not the enhancement of the common weal, that dictated the spirit of imperialism, but the greed of private interests, the desire for profit on the part of aggressive elements influential enough to have the support of their governments. And since their only object was the most profit in the shortest possible time, the uttermost farthing to the bitterest end, of course they would not ameliorate the lot of those who incidentally had to be subjugated, of course they would grant no concessions until wrung from them by the blood-cry of frenzied mobs. When they yielded they had to yield. That is to say, the government at home could not pledge the support of the people for a colonial war for "disciplinary measures." This kind of imperialism being the premise, the conclusion is the philosophy of force.

The period of tutelage in the backward areas is not yet over. With the exception of Japan, which is itself an empire, there is not a country in Asia or Africa capable of efficiently functioning as an industrialized society. Left to their own devices they would progress slowly, if they did not stand still or regress. Now the empires are in chastened mood and would compromise. Ideally, compromise is still the best solution. But now compromise is unacceptable. Now our willingness to compromise is imputed to weakness. Reforms are offered too late to earn good will or to bespeak sincerity. We ask the Chinese to wait until they have made their transition, until they have replaced a corrupt mandarinate by an honest and efficient civil service, and educated the population to a sense of political responsibility. We ask the Indians to wait until they have levelled the mountainous barriers of caste, composed the internal religious enmities, and welded national unity out of their heterogeneous elements. We shall be asking the Nicaraguans, Haitians and Santo Dominicans to wait until they have learned how to effect a change in government without a revolution.

They will not wait unless they have to. The rancors are ingrained now and suspicion is ineradicable. Why should our promises be accepted at face value? They have been heard before. What nation, on landing troops somewhere to preserve law and order, has not solemnly proclaimed to the world that the occupation was only temporary and for the purpose of restoring law and order, after which it would be withdrawn? And what nation has ever withdrawn? What reason is there to believe that any great Power ever will voluntarily release any of its territorial possessions unless thrown out?

America says it will free the Philippines when the Filipinos are ready for self-government. But the tests of fitness for self-government are not laid down in advance. America remains tribunal; and America's judgment will be affected by its own material interests. And America's judgment will not be delivered by the masses of the American people who have no material interest at stake, but by the small minority that has. The decision of this minority will always be cast in the direction of its own advantage. As Filipinos become more apt in the arts of government, as more and more of the rising generation come under the influence of American schools and the tradition of representative government, the higher we shall then push the standards applicable to Filipino capacity. In fact, the elevation in standard will be in equal measure with the increase in Filipino capacity. It is more logical to predict that the longer America stays in the Philippines the less likely it is to get out. For the greater will be its economic interest. Suppose the efforts made at intervals to strike oil are successful; suppose that rubber is grown on a large scale and the American automobile tire manufacturer no longer has to pay monopoly prices to the British grower; can anyone seriously believe that the United States will be more likely then to loose the bonds of the Philippines than it is now?

This over-driven phrase, "fitness for self-government," must be examined a little more closely. None of the now dependent nations, it is true, is capable of exercising good government. Is America? If the capacity to govern efficiently, wisely and honestly is the determinant of a nation's right to self-rule, is there any country in the world entitled to independence, with the possible exception of England? It may be granted that the dependent peoples fall far below the standard of the politically advanced—that is, those more expert in the arts of representative government, which happens to be congenial to the Anglo-Saxon empirical temperament. Even by their own standards, however, the dependent peoples fail. The Chinese military mandarinate is corrupt and incompetent and without sense of public duty. The old Egyptian tax collectors were leeches on the peasantry. In Korea a peasant was afraid to have more than one work animal lest the local official conclude that he was wealthy and proceed to extort from him under the guise of taxes.

It may be laid down as an axiom that no nation will introduce reforms, will purge itself of its social poisons, while under alien oppression. The house will never be set in order while a mighty intruder stalks through its rooms. In the first place, the alien intruder wants the house in disorder. In an ordered establishment he could pick up less of value and his place as an unbidden guest would be insecure. Let any of the inhabitants, wearying of slovenliness, seriously propose house-cleaning, and the foreigner busily sets himself to prevent a beginning. With moral influence he supports those who hold that the good old mess was good enough for them. With more material influence he supports those who wish to oust the utopians who fly in the face of the proved wisdom of experience. In fact, very often the opposition to house-cleaning is underwritten entirely by the foreigner, who simultaneously and in all sincerity lectures the inhabitants on the necessity of good housekeeping, and proclaims to the neighborhood at large that in the interval he will remain in the house to protect the valuables for the good of the inhabitants themselves.

In the second place, there is something demoralizing in being subjected to foreign conquest. The stigma of inferiority attaches itself, however vigorously it may be repudiated and bitterly resented. It is dispiriting. There is no incentive to bestir oneself on one's own behalf when one is subordinated to an overwhelming power from without. What use is there? One is not the master of one's fate anyway. Final decision will rest with the power from without in any case. Little opportunity is given for the exercise by which alone proficiency is gained. Natives are allowed to serve as hewers of wood and drawers of water in the bureaucracy. Young sprigs of the ruling race fresh from home and inexperienced are given higher posts when there are vacancies. The native is allowed no chance to get experience in positions of responsibility.

In the third place, the presence of an alien invader or the threat of invasion is an asset to the corrupt native official. He can always draw a red herring across the trail of his own malfeasance. When the populace begins to pry embarrassingly and becomes incensed, he can always turn off wrath to fall on the foreigner. It is a device not restricted to backward countries. Respectable countries have been known to stifle unrest at home by adventurings abroad and the consequent rallying to patriotism.

WHAT MIGHT HAVE BEEN

In the fourth place, if a country has not yet been subdued but is only under the menace of foreign encroachment, its educated classes are too occupied with devising measures to keep the country out of foreign clutches for any serious attention to domestic problems. Turkey is the perfect example. If Turkey were to allot a more generous share of its slender budget to schools or agricultural improvements or roads, the army would have to be reduced. And if Turkey's power of resistance were weakened to an appreciable extent, the wolves of Europe would be at its throat. The men of the new régime in Angora are well aware of domestic needs but must subordinate them to the prior claim of survival. If a country is already under alien domination, the energies of its people will be absorbed and their attention concentrated in hatred of the alien enemy. Every question is crossed by the foreign issue, as in Ireland until a few years ago men divided only according to their attitude toward England. They divided on the proposition to buy a fire hose according to the proponent's known stand for or against England. No public question can be argued out and settled on its intrinsic merits. Domestic concerns, though touching the population more intimately than the status of national sovereignty, are dwarfed by the fact of foreign rule.

It is said with monotonous frequency and with stereotyped uniformity that if China, for example, will but take thought to itself, rid itself of the incubus of bandit-generals and decadent mandarins, and under the leadership of an adequate government attain full strength, no foreign Power can molest it. The foreign problem of China will solve itself automatically if the Chinese will but look to their domestic problems. That is indisputable. The masses of Chinese suffer far more from their grafting officialdom than from the derogations put upon them by a few thousand foreigners on the fringes of their country. The Szechuenese peasant has never heard of extraterritoriality. But he has directly experienced the looting of his house by soldiery running loose in one general's private war with another general for the privilege of bilking the neighborhood. Yet the Chinese fulminate in hysterical monomania in their anti-foreignism and give little heed to their own ills.

It is illogical, quite. But men are not logical. The mainsprings of their actions are in their emotions. The foreigners' abuses may be less injurious than those inflicted by one's compatriots, but they hurt more because they strike a more sensitive area. It may be illogical, but it is universal; and when the phenomenon is observed frequently enough and in all conditions, a formula must once be constructed— a formula which must be taken as a postulate of international policy and action. Platitudinous it may be but also true, that any people prefers being miserably governed by itself to being well governed by another people. The instinct may also be a sound one, for if each group remains master of its fate it may reshape its fate when and as desired. When a callow and overheated Filipino student shouts that he wants Americans out so that his own elected officials can govern him, it is futile to try to prove to him from the record what his own officials are like whereas American rule is honestly administered—more honestly, in fact, than in America. It is futile to direct appeals to his reason, because his reason does not dictate his beliefs. He is prompted by something underlying reason and perhaps equally valid as motive. But his attitude and the attitude of other Filipinos—and of Chinese and Hindus and Egyptians and Nicaraguans—is a fact, an unchangeable fact and to be accepted as such, whether regrettable or not.

Before proceeding I wish to make an observation with regard to dishonesty in government, on which there is so much emphasis in any discussion of the relations between the West and the East. The political venality of the East is truly appalling. To one from more decorous parts it is revolting. But after one has lived long in the East and then returned home and looked about him with eyes afresh, horror is somewhat modulated. The political corruption of the East is shocking because it is direct, crude and visible. It consists of purchase and sale of public office, giving and taking of bribes, and the diversion to an official's pocket of a percentage of all public moneys passing through his hands. In the more respectable countries of Europe and America corruption is indirect, subtle, and more difficult to recognize. It is a matter not of bribery but of conferring privilege on the favored few—not denying that in the United States there is bribery too. I am not sure where and under which form of corruption the people are mulcted more. I am inclined to believe that on a dollars-and-cents calculation the Chinese, Persian and Turkish peasant comes off cheaper than the farmer in Indiana. Consider the manipulation of tariff legislation in the United States. There are no bribes, no legally punishable offenses are committed. But is it honest? And what does it cost the American consumer? Is he unjustly and dishonestly deprived of much less of his income than the Near Eastern shopkeeper who must part with a few cents baksheesh to get a shipment through the customs? England is admittedly the most uprightly administered country in the world. Yet the influence of landed proprietors, mine owners and bankers at the seat of government is notorious. An analogy may be found in the comparison between the dime-pinching on contracts by the henchmen of our numerous urban Tammany Halls and the discreet deals between perfect gentlemen in chastely appointed luncheon clubs where public utilities franchises worth millions are arranged, sheltered from the prying gaze of the public which will pay. One is uglier and more vulgar but to the taxpayer much cheaper.

The period of tutelage for the materially backward nations is not over. Much could be gained by its prolongation, much lost by its curtailment, but I said in the beginning and must repeat: the whole question of the welfare of our subject nationalities must be excluded in any consideration of the practical problems arising in imperialism. Certainly we have conferred material benefits on the backward peoples we have conquered. The Chinese merchant in the International Settlement in Shanghai enjoys security of property envied by his compatriots under Chinese jurisdiction thirty miles away. There are fewer revolutions in Haiti since the American occupation. If the United States never evacuates Nicaragua fewer Nicaraguans will lose their lives in senseless biennial civil wars. Wherever we have set foot on the Caribbean shores we are severing the population's bondage to disease. If the United States should go into Mexico, in time banditry will not be a normal institution and the peon's standard of living will be incomparably higher. Much has been taken from our subject nationalities, and much given in return; and of the latter much will be lost if the ruling nations voluntarily retire or are driven out. For the time, at least, there will be relapse.

Under the circumstances would it not be unfortunate to leave the subject nationalities to their own devices? Would it not be a matter of regret even to one who is not acquisitive and dislikes the principle of conquest? Can we, indeed, evade the responsibility, once having undertaken it? Futile questions now! Now the only question is, can we help leaving them to their own devices? It might have been possible to fulfill our responsibility had the imperial Powers originally followed the counsel of perfection sketched earlier in this chapter. They did not. Now it is too late.

Those who can benefit from that which we have to give have been compelled to take also that which is intolerable. The good in imperialism has been linked indisseverably with the evil. Since the good is accidental and the evil deliberate, and the good is apparent only in long perspective while the evil is felt directly and immediately, offense at the evil has overborne gratitude for the good. The system in which the two are linked is challenged. The welfare of the subject peoples must now be considered as a question apart. The issues which confront us out of imperialism must be solved according to our own welfare and examined from that point of view alone.

CHAPTER XVI

CONCLUSION: DILEMMA

FROM the point of view solely of our own good, our own highest interest, what shall we of the ruling nations do? Better, what can we do? For most likely we shall do nothing, but wait for events to overwhelm us. So it has been always in the past, in the international conflicts among ourselves as well as in our relations with subject nationalities. Causes are recognized after their effects have begun to flow; wisdom comes in retrospect. While we erect memorials to the dead and clear away the ruins, historians with profound researches solemnly discover that which was obvious before it became history. Reflecting ruefully on the import of their discoveries, we set our faces anew in the same direction and move forward to the same destination, eyes open and unseeing.

So it is in Europe now after 1918. So all the indications are that it will be in the larger conflict between Europe and the United States, on the one hand, and the continents they have laid in subjection in the process of empire, on the other. The stage of history has broadened. Its drama promises to be played out with larger figures, driven by more ponderous forces. The action turns no longer on the clash of nation and nation in Europe, sundered by ancient animosities, but on the clash of continents, systems, races and civilizations in antagonisms fired by the most inflammable of elements, racial passions. The climax is as yet but dimly visible. Whether the end will be tragedy is still to be determined.

There are no signs of conscious effort to avert the usual end. There are no signs of recognition that we are moving in the same direction. We have reached the climax in China. We have been drawing toward it for years. All that has taken place in China is as the working out of a mathematical formula; it has been mathematically predictable. We let ourselves drift nevertheless. In the spring of 1927 we stood, British and American armies on one side of barricades in Shanghai, Chinese armies on the other. There was miraculous deliverance from catastrophe then. The climax passed, but the causes remain. The formula still holds and it is still mathematically predictable that the effects will be the same. They will bring us to climax again. Army will confront army again, but miracles do not recur endlessly. Meanwhile we remain placidly at status quo ante, as if there had never been a climax, taking no steps to remove the causes, unwilling to face them or oblivious of them, presumably waiting to survey them in retrospect among the ruins. Where it has not yet come to climax, as notably in India, we let the causes take form. Where there are no causes yet, we create them, as in Mexico. It is as if there were no past, the present were not big in our eyes, and the future would not be.

Let it be assumed, however, that the faculty of foresight is not denied to men, and that they are capable of learning from experience and ordering their conduct in international relations at least as rationally as in their personal business relations. There is slight evidence for the assumption, but it must be made, if only as an act of faith; by any other we resign ourselves to serve as the sport of fate, an abdication contrary to every postulate on which our lives are founded. Suppose, then, that instead of waiting for events to overwhelm us we were to survey this situation as it confronts us, determined rationally to seek a solution that best serves our interest. The situation is this: We have empire, we want empire, we need empire. Our dependencies refuse to remain dependent. They want to be freed. Naturally we do not want to free them. What, concretely, shall we do?

The necessity for decision cannot be evaded. It will not present itself from all the dependencies at once, of course. The time will vary with local conditions. In nearly all of Africa it can be postponed for long, as it can be wherever there are primitive cultures and an embryonic sense of unity. In North

Africa, especially Egypt, postponement will not be for long. In possessions with a small population there will be no immediate critical urgency. They can at best conduct irredentist campaigns, with sporadic outbursts of violence, an everrunning undercurrent of disaffection, and deposits of tinder beneath the surface ready for ignition by the most fleeting spark. Theirs will be a nuisance value, but Ireland has proved how ponderable this can be. The Philippine Islands, with their 12,000,000 inhabitants, can not wage open war against the United States, neither can Haiti or Nicaragua. They can compel us to maintain large garrisons and periodically send out punitive and disciplinary expeditions. They can make our tenure so expensive, in money and energy, that the coldest material calculation will show a debit balance. The power of resistance of a disgruntled subject nationality should not be underestimated. Though negative, it works out to the same effect from our point of view as a more weighty antagonist.

Where there are cultural identity, consciousness of unity, organized nationalism and patriotism intensified by repression and frustration, there postponement cannot be looked for. Peculiar local factors, such as lack of homogeneity in India, may work in our favor, but not decisively. They only change the form of the crisis produced; it may be in an ascending scale of revolts rather than a single blow for emancipation. Taking the long view, there is no

CONCLUSION: DILEMMA

evasion. There have been enough uprisings in the last ten years to offer conclusive evidence. What we stem now returns soon, reinvigorated and with greater momentum. The longer we evade the more likely is initiative to pass from us, the more likely we are to be compelled to fight whether we want to or not, whether the thing is worth fighting for or not. I am not dealing with time in journalistic measurement. I do not mean war in twelve weeks or twelve months. On the other hand, it may very well be twelve weeks or six weeks. China, outwardly somnolent in 1924, flared in 1925 and in 1927 was the center of world attention. India, outwardly somnolent early in 1927, may flare late in 1927. Insurgency in the Philippines, slowly gathering for a decade, may burst into action without forewarning, hastened by some trivial incident or by an accident.

Taking the long view, also, there is no practical possibility of compromise. Ideally there is, and if this were merely an intellectual exercise a happy solution could be found. If there were ten real statesmen at the helm of governments in the principal countries of Europe and in the United States, if among the financial and industrial potentates of those countries there were ten men who could see beyond the year's balance sheet, then there might be compromise. We could make detached survey of conditions within our empires, coolly estimate what they demand or are likely to demand, and then, in order to placate them and thus hold them, offer them just a little more. We should make the grand gesture to China, and voluntarily and without negotiation announce that henceforth we let China fix its own tariff, we renounce extraterritoriality as of even date, we withdraw our gunboats from China's inland waters and our troops from its cities, and we solemnly covenant to make retrocession of the foreign concessions and settlements by January 1, 1951; but we ask China to be tolerant in its assumption of jurisdiction and to make the transfer as easy to us as possible. Thus we might salve something out of the wreckage. In India, before the time for revision of the Montagu-Chelmsford plan, the British would inform the Indian National Congress that on January 1, 1940, India would assume the status of Dominion home rule, and that in preparation therefor there would be a graduated relinquishment of British authority, beginning with immediate equal representation for Indians in executive councils and elective Indian majorities in legislative assemblies, in which would be vested jurisdiction over all affairs of government.

This is begging the question: the counsel of perfection again. If there were in Europe and America ten real statesmen and ten financial and industrial potentates whose imagination went beyond immediate profit, we should not be in a situation where we had to make such sacrifices. Even so it is doubtful

CONCLUSION: DILEMMA

whether such a compromise would not be postponement rather than solution. Against the background which has been built over decades, quite likely it would be only a stimulant to more extreme intransigence. It might serve as emollient and ease the transition to both sides, but the end would be the same. For all practical purposes there is no compromise.

Thinking now not in terms of to-day and tomorrow but in historical terms, our choice is to cut loose or fight. Eventually—it may be next year in one place and twenty years from now in another—we must either free our dependencies voluntarily, seeking only to anæsthetize the surgery or graduate the severance, or must hold them by force. Which shall it be? Which offers the greater gain or the smaller loss? The test, of course, is economic. National honor or prestige will not keep us where it does not pay to stay; where it pays us enough to stay, we shall if we can, even if national honor and prestige are not involved. What is at stake?

First, trade. I believe it to be certain that if by some event beyond our control our imperial possessions were loosed to-morrow, our trade would suffer seriously, at least for a time. Our trade in such areas has been built up on a basis of autonomy, of complete immunity from local authority, of prior rights. Remove the guaranty of autonomy and substitute native jurisdiction and immediately we should be subject to a multitude of hindrances, some deliberate and some inevitable in the circumstances. The shelter we enjoyed from local inefficiency and instability would be removed. In the transition to independence normal channels would be blocked or diverted, normal processes interrupted. There would be deliberate obstructions inflicted by the native people newly come to power, just to prove that they had the power. Annoying taxes would be imposed, needless formalities of routine insisted upon, ceremonial deferences exacted. Old scores would be paid off with interest. It was so in Japan after foreign restrictions were removed, it was conspicuously so in Turkey after 1923. It would be so everywhere. A people long deprived of power when newly restored to it will exercise it for its own sake, even abuse it, if only to convince themselves that they really have it. Without such demonstration they cannot feel certain of their accession.

In the interval of adjustment, which might be long or short, our commerce would be adversely affected. What does this represent in figures? The exports of the United States in 1924 totalled $4,300,000,000. Of this sum more than half represents exports to Europe, approximately fifteen per cent to Canada and seven per cent to South America. In other words, three-quarters of our exports went to countries not imperialistically controlled. Of the balance, $560,000,000 went to Asia, $440,000,000 to Mexico, Central America and all the West Indies, $157,000,000

CONCLUSION: DILEMMA

to the oceanic islands, and $64,000,000 to Africa. The United Kingdom, buying $900,000,000 worth of goods, took almost as much of our products as Asia, Mexico, Central America and the islands in the Caribbean. Our exports to Central America, Cuba, Porto Rico, Hawaii and the Philippines, our principal outlying possessions and spheres, totalled $455,000,000, a little more than ten per cent of the whole. If the profit on our $6,000,000 bill to Nicaragua were one hundred per cent, it would still fall far short of paying the upkeep of the Marines there. To the United States the imperial dependencies are not a very vital concern in commerce.

To England the trade of the dependencies means much more, not counting now the self-governing Dominions as dependencies. Even so, more than half the exports of the United Kingdom go to continental Europe and the United States, and roughly about one-quarter to the dependencies. So much is England's welfare bound up with foreign trade, however, that the loss of even a minor fraction is of grave consequence. The closing of the Indian market would add markedly to unemployment in Lancashire, the boycott against British goods in South China was instantly felt in the English industrial centers. Also these figures are oversimplified. Foreign trade is intricately involved. It is not only a two-sided transaction. If England were to lose its trade with India it could not buy so much from the United

States; the United States could not then buy so much from France; France could not then buy so much from England. England therefore would lose more than its trade with India if it lost its trade with India.

On the other hand there is no reason to believe that all England's exports to India would fall off immediately and that in time they would not be recovered. It is as likely that in time England would get even more of India's trade than when India was governed from London. Under imperialistic control the development of a market may be hindered as much as advanced. Where there is not exclusive control by one Power it is certain to be hindered. The rivalry of numerous Powers, each striving for a monopoly, expresses itself in the dog-in-the-manger policy. Whole regions are left untapped by railroads because no Power will permit any other to have the privilege of constructing them. The development of the market is therefore retarded and all lose alike.

Where there is exclusive control by one Power it does not follow that there will not be the dog-in-the-manger policy, too, though working within the country. To develop a market in the Philippines, for instance, certain steps have to be taken. But what steps are taken in practice—those which will create a market for all American trade or those which will be to the advantage of a few corporations already having vested interests and desiring a monopoly? Are India's possibilities cultivated with a view to the

CONCLUSION: DILEMMA

profits of the two or three British banking groups entrenched in India and their affiliates, or to the benefit of all Manchester and Birmingham? It is true that the home government makes the decision as to what steps shall be taken, but who influences the home government—in the informal, after-dinner manner by which influence is exerted? I doubt whether there is ground for the assumption that in establishing hegemony over a backward country we proceed as a national economic unit, having in mind the good of the national whole.

This brings us to the basic fallacy of examining questions like this from the point of view of the national economy, as if in practice there were such an entity. It may be demonstrated quite conclusively that in commerce, at least, imperialism does not pay. Pay whom? In proportion to the whole of foreign trade, trade with areas under imperial control does not bulk large; even in the case of England not so large that the loss of trade with imperial possessions would be ruinous. Figured per capita of the population, it may even be inconsiderable. It cannot be figured per capita for practical, realistic purposes. The profits are not spread per capita nor would the losses be. The profits are the stake of certain corporate interests, and so are the losses. In practical politics, in the influence which guides the decisions of governments and pledges the action of populations, the profits and losses of these corporate interests are what matter. The $125,000,000 worth of goods that the United States exports to China in a year, if lost entirely, would affect the income of the average man very little, even assuming that there would be a proportionate loss in employment, which is not inevitable. But it would affect very much the Standard Oil Company of New York, which has a large share of the $125,000,000. In the politics of imperialism the Standard Oil companies, not the national economy, count.

More important than foreign trade is the question of raw materials. Here our dependence on regions under imperial control is more direct and vital. I have already elaborated the point that to keep our industrial machinery in operation we must have raw materials, and that in so far as we must look to undeveloped areas for those materials we must control those areas, for their inhabitants cannot extract them themselves. Now it is exaggerating to say that the West could never have industrialized without the raw materials of Asia, Africa and the oceanic islands. As a matter of fact, the West did. But the catapulted progress of the last fifty years would never have been realized unless we had been able to tap new supplies when our own were beginning to run low. Our industrialization would have been retarded. It cannot be said that without continued access to the stores in backward regions our industry would come to a standstill now. But our industrial system is organized

CONCLUSION: DILEMMA

on the basis of unimpeded access to raw materials everywhere and of the exploitation of deposits known but not yet tapped. To have these sources suddenly shut off to us would impede industry, compel it to reorganize, and therefore compel our society to reorganize, and change the physical aspect of our daily lives. The writer quoted in the preface, who said that without imperialism we could not have automobiles because gasoline and tires would be too dear, was not being rhetorical. We should be deprived of many other commodities, or they would become so dear as to be luxuries to a large proportion of us. This does not mean that there are so many basic materials which are to be found only in imperially controlled lands and which would therefore be denied to us entirely if we lost our empires, but only that we are becoming dependent on the supplementary stores to be found in such lands and our dependence will increase as our own stores are exhausted.

Oil is still plentiful in the United States, but the world demand can be satisfied only if the petroleum resources of Mexico, Persia, the Dutch East Indies and Mesopotamia are made available. The struggle among the international oil syndicates for command of the wells in those regions is not based on the needs of to-day but on the needs of twenty years hence. Unless they can be assured of continued supplies they must begin to retrench now. Copper is to be found in the United States, but the Belgian Congo and Mexico are also being drawn on and must continue to be. For tin we must look almost entirely to the British Malay possessions, the Dutch East Indies and Bolivia, with additional supplies from China and Nigeria. Without our imperial possessions we should be deprived entirely of rubber, nearly all of which is grown in the British and Dutch possessions in southeastern Asia. Copra, palm oil, chromite, graphite, jute, camphor and quinine are taken in large part from our dependencies, as are more than half of the world's supply of cocoa, tea, shellac, wool and long-staple cotton.

It may be that synthetic substitutes for raw materials, such as are being successfully experimented with in Germany, may solve the problem by nullifying it. If not, it remains insoluble. A large share of the raw materials of the world is to be found in territories now parts of the Western empires; and the resources of some of the more remote and inaccessible regions are as yet untouched. If we are to have the use of them, these territories must remain parts of Western empires, not of this or that empire necessarily but under supervision of a technologically competent nation. The alternative is serious loss, primarily to great manufacturing corporations but in this case filtering down much more widely, and in addition a readjustment in production: how far-reaching it is difficult to estimate.

Theoretically, socially, the focal point is the ques-

CONCLUSION: DILEMMA

tion of raw materials. It is there we strike the balance between gain and loss in coming to the decision whether to hold empire or renounce it. Practically the focal point is not raw materials so much as financial vested interest—the exportation of capital. It is incontestable that without continued imperialistic control the money invested in materially backward and politically unstable lands will be insecure. Without continued imperialistic control we shut off opportunities for the loans and bond issues at high rates of interest to construct railways, open mines, dig petroleum wells and establish banks in countries not yet come to mechanization, those which constitute the prizes of imperialism. We cannot send money into Central America without following it with Marines. As a matter of fact we have sent little without following it with Marines. Then more money has gone in after the Marines, thus affording additional reason why we must keep the Marines there. Here the chasm cannot be spanned. Either we deny to those of our citizens who have capital to export the right to export it where they can reap the handsomest return, or we must give them the protection of our military forces and superimpose our own authority over local authority at least to the extent of extraterritorial protection. To whatever materially retarded region our capital goes, there empire must go. Where money has gone and empire is lost, it is certain in nine cases out of ten that money is lost too.

Whose money? In part, those to whom foreign bonds have been passed down after the floating syndicates have taken off a handsome commission for underwriting and service. Among them will be many who have sunk their savings. But those to whom the biggest profits have gone and to whom the biggest profits will go if the system is unbroken are banking groups, investment syndicates, and industrial amalgamations. Theirs is the big stake in imperialism. But they are the dominant elements in our social system, and it is a foundation stone of our social system that these groups shall suffer no inhibition and that private property has an inalienable right to make as much as it can anywhere. Where it goes, though to make money for itself, it carries the collective might of a whole nation, delivered through the nation's government, to support it in exercise of the right. So long as this principle infuses our thinking and is the premise of our social ordering, our governments are not only consistent but in duty bound to "protect life and property" without asking whether the life should have been there except at its own risk, or what, or whose, the property is and how acquired. Our governments must, though undeliberately and unconsciously, set out on the course of empire. They have and they will. Not out of villainy or wilful betrayal of the rights of the mass of the people in the interests of the favored few, but out of every tenet of the philosophy of their social system.

CONCLUSION: DILEMMA

I see no reason to cavil at them or to denounce imperialism as a poisonous, exotic growth that must be uprooted. It is rather a natural growth, rooted in soil to which it is indigenous.

It is a fallacy to draw any balance sheet for imperialism, with the cost of armaments and wars on one side and the return in trade, raw materials and profits on investments on the other. By such a casting of accounts it is of course transparent that imperialism does not pay. To send 200,000 men with warships and airplanes and munitions to put down Chinese nationalism so that we can retain our imperialistic privileges, is to pay a premium of $500 on a fire insurance policy of $1,000. But this assumes erringly that those who enjoy the profits of the imperialistic privileges are those who also pay the cost of the war, whereas the cost of the war is divided pro rata among the population while the profits are not. It assumes, also erringly, that we can dispense with the raw materials, whereas we cannot dispense with them without taking a step in devolution. To strike such a balance is unreal.

Taking forethought, then, to our situation, we find that voluntarily to renounce imperialism requires us to alter the structure of our industrialized society and to recast a fundamental premise of our social philosophy. It is highly doubtful whether it is possible to do the first, and equally improbable that we shall be willing to try. There is no sign of any inclination to do the second. It is highly doubtful, therefore, whether we can renounce imperialism and equally improbable that we shall do so voluntarily. On the other hand, the subject nationalities in our empires challenge our imperialism. Since the past cannot be undone, though now we see its errors, there does not seem to be possibility of compromise. But the alternative, to hold these subject nationalities by force, will not only cost more than is to be gained, but may subject our social fabric to a strain that it can hardly support. Even then the ultimate outcome is questionable. Matching force against force, we can, of course, subdue the Chinese, Indians, Filipinos, Mexicans, Egyptians and Syrians. But it might be a Pyrrhic victory. The inexorable law of history is witness that a conquest so imposed cannot forever endure.

We of the Western empires appear to be in the position of the gentleman in the Chinese adage who is riding a tiger. He does not want to stay on and he dare not get off. It is not revealed how he took his mount. No doubt, like ourselves, he was constrained by a situation beyond his control. More prosaically, we are caught in a dilemma and we shall have to seize either horn. It would be presumptuous to offer instruction and advice. The factors determining the decision lie in the future, still undefined. But since it is probable that we shall come to it in the end in any

CONCLUSION: DILEMMA

event, the preponderance of discernible evidence seems to be in favor of seizing the one which will take us out entirely. The cost will be dire; there need be no self-deception on that score. But it is probably the smaller cost of the two between which we must choose. Above all, our best hope lies in making the decision while it is still ours to make: either consciously, on full deliberation and knowing why, rigorously to suppress the rebellious subject nationalities, now when the initiative is ours and there is more likelihood that we can; or at once to get about the business of liquidation and cut them loose, now when there is more likelihood that the surgery will not be fatal to ourselves.

INDEX

Addison, Joseph, 43
Aguinaldo, 223, 225
Allah, 227
Allied *cordon sanitaire*, 270
  Powers, 139, 186, 251
Allies, 187, 189, 191
America and imperialism, 216-249
American, club, 146
  Revolution, 130
Amherst, Lord, 41
Anglo-Japanese alliance, 62
Anglo-Russian feud, 101
Annam, Emperor of, 51
Attila, 21
"Autobiography," Mark Twain, 225
"Awakening of Asia, The," Henry M. Hyndman, 37

Balance of power, 54, 55
Balkan wars, 121, 128
Bannerman, Campbell, 258
Battle of Adowa, 124
Birkenhead, Lord, 250, 253, 269
Boer War, 119, 123, 257-258
Bolshevik Red Russian, 192
Boxer Movement, 58
  Rebellion, 252, 267
British Concession in China, 250
  in Hankow, 250
  East India Company, 40, 45, 99
  Legation, 60
  South Africa Company, 110
Bryan-Chamorro treaty, 242
Bryan, Secretary, 242

Bunau-Varilla, Philippe, 235

Caperton, Admiral, 238
Chamorro, General, 240, 242
Central Powers, 138
Chamberlain, Austen, 260
  Joseph, 107, 108, 132
Chartered Company of Rhodesia, 109
Chesterfield, 148
Ch'ien Lung, Emperor, 40, 42
China-Japan War, 120
China, perfect illustration of imperialism in, 33-65
Chinese Nationalism, 64, 232, 250, 303
Christendom, 197, 198, 199
Christianity, 133-134, 172-173, 187, 196, 197, 199, 251
Churchill, Winston, 133
Civil War of 1850, in China, 55
Cleveland, President, 222
Cochin China, war over, 51
Co-hongs, 41
Colonialism, 32
Committee of Public Safety, 221, 222
Communist uprisings in 1926 in Java and Sumatra, 266
Confucius, 148
  golden rule of, 10
Conquistadores, new style, 21
Coolidge, Calvin, President, 224, 243, 257
Council of the Secretary of State, in India, 258
  of the Viceroy, in India, 258

[307]

Creel, George, 188
Crimean War, 119
Cromer, Lord, Evelyn Baring, 115
Crowder, General E. H., 233
Curzon, Lord, 254

Daily Mail, 69
Daimyos, 149
Dawson Pact, 241
"Defenders of Islamic Asia," 138
De Lesseps Company, 235
Democracy, 128, 129, 130, 131, 134, 135, 140, 151, 187, 221, 239
Dewey, Admiral, 223
    John, 203
Dey of Algeria, 105
Diaz, Adolfo, 241, 242, 246
    Adolpho, 243
    Porfirio, 244, 245
Disraeli, 100
Dollar diplomacy, 230
Dominicans, 35
Dyer, General, 254

Eastern dependencies, 253
    faiths, 198
    nationalism, 137
    territories, 257
East India Company, 100, 258
East, the, 91, 99, 139, 144, 148, 150, 161, 168, 176, 177, 194, 195, 197, 200, 206, 250, 251, 254, 261, 263, 270, 275, 283
"Economic Imperialism," Leonard Woolf, 110
Egyptian nationalism, 114
    outbreak of 1882, 114
El-Krim, Abd, 265
Elks Club, Manila, 151
Entente, the, 120

Estrada-Chamorro-Diaz revolution, 241
Estrada, Juan, 240
Evelyn Baring, Lord Cromer, 115
Evolution, 158, 205, 212, 273

Far East, 53, 63, 120, 178, 179, 192, 232, 262, 263
Far Eastern politics, 78
Fourteen Points, 188
France, Anatole, 203
Franciscans, 35
French and American Revolutions, 17-18
    Concession, in China, 165
    Revolution, 128, 129-130
Fundamentalism, 173

Gandhi, 144, 165, 195, 213, 269
    movement, 93, 258
George, Lloyd, 175, 251
George III, 42
Goethe, 203
Gokhale, 145
Golden Age, 213, 226
    rule of Confucius, 10
Gordon, 123
Gospels, the, 198
    of Jesus, 197, 199
"Grand Seigneur," 138
Grey, Earl, 109
    Sir Edward, 121

Harding administration, 259
Harrimans, interests of, 231
Hearst, William Randolph, 204
Hebrew-Christian ideology, 199
Huerta, 246
Hussein, King of Hedjaz, 266
Hyndman, Henry M., "The Awakening of Asia," 37

INDEX

Illinois Central bonds, 78
Imperialism, 4-19, 20, 28, 32, 217
  and America, 216-249
  and the industrial system, 82-98
  and the World War, 183-193
  causes of native's change of attitude toward, 128-216
  conclusion, 287-305
  in China, 33-65
  motives of, 66-81
  personal equation in, 157-182
  reaction of the native to, 118-127
  reckoning of, 250-270
  results of, 99-117
  what might have been, 271-286
Imperialistic aggression, 186-187, 255
  control, 95, 296
  domination, 85
  era, 184
  expansion, 214, 216
  privileges, 303
  rivalries, 118
Imperial possessions, 120
Independence party, 154
Independencista leaders, 257
Indian Mutiny, 100
  nationalism, 12
Industrialism, 76, 92, 210, 211, 212, 214, 275
Industrial Revolution, 73, 129
  system, 82, 196, 205
Inquisition, 36
International settlement, 165
  in Shanghai, 285
Ismail, 113

Jameson, Dr., 110
Jesuits, 35
Jewish colony, of Honan, 37
John Hay, 61
Johnson, Dr., 43
Jones Bill, 225

Kellogg, Frank B., Secretary, 133, 260
Kemal, Mustapha, 139, 262
Khan, Jenghis, 21
Kitchener, Lord, 115, 123, 254
Knox, Secretary, 231, 240
Korean War, 52

Laborites, 175-176
League of Nations, 266
  Mandate Commission, 266
Leopold II, 107, 108
Libertarians, 176
Liliuokalani, Queen, 221
Lin Tse-hsü, 46
Lippmann, Walter, 118
Liquidation, 1-19, 305
Lo Bengula, 111

Macartney, Lord, 41
Machiavelli, 203
Madero, 245
Madriz, José, 240, 241
Madero revolution, 245
Magna Carta, 132
Mahdist uprising, 123
Manchurian railways, 231
Mayfair, 177
McKinley, President, 222, 224, 227
  tariff bill, 221
Medean law, 149
Mexican Constitution of 1917, Article 27, 247, 248
  nationals, 247, 248
  peon, 245, 285
  revolutions, 246
West, 207
Western Americans, 178

Millin, Sarah Gertrude, "The South Africans," 144-145
Monroe Doctrine, 219, 233
Montagu, Edwin S., 189, 258
Montagu-Chelmsford plan, 269, 292
  reforms, 258
Morocco crises (1906, 1911), 120
Moscow Antichrist, 17

Napoleonic wars, 102
National Bank of Haiti, 239
  of Nicaragua, 241
  City Bank of New York, 238, 239
  Railroad, 239
Nationalism, 128, 129, 130, 131, 134, 135, 140, 156, 265, 268, 290
Nationalist party, 139
Nationalistic Movement, 266
Nationalists, 138, 139, 153, 265
Native reaction to imperialism, effect of the war, 183-193
  seeds of discontent, 128-140
  seeds of hatred, 141-156
  skepticism with regard to superiority of our civilization, 194-215
Near East, 178, 262
Nicholas II, 270
Non-coöperative movement in India, 269
North Manchuria Railway, 53

Occident, 130, 268
Occidental, the, 197
  educational system, 203
Occidentals, 213
Ohio Republicanism, 228
Open Door, 61, 219, 229, 230, 231, 235

Opium, 44-45, 50
  war, 47
Oriental, the, 208, 253
Osmena, Sergio, 222, 257
Outpost, mind, 179
  phrases, 184

Panther, 120
Paris Peace Conference, 259, 265
Paul, apostle, 203
Peking and Hankow Railway, 55
  club, 148
Perry, Commodore, 52
Personal equation, 157, 162, 165
Philippine rebellion, 124
  revolution (1790), 222
  three years' war, 225
"Pickwickian independence," 233
Platt Amendment, 233, 234
Polo, Marco, 35, 43

Quezon, Manuel, 222, 257

Rasputin, 270
Rebellion of 1837 in Canada, 258
Republic, of China established, 63
Revolt in Panama, 235
  of South American colonies against Spain, 128
Revolution in Haiti, 238
  in Nicaragua, 240
Rhodes, Cecil, 109, 110, 116, 132
Rizal, José, 222-223
Roosevelt, President, 237
Roxas, Manuel, 222, 257
Royal Dutch-Shell Company, 88

INDEX

"Ruler of Nations," 224, 227
Russell, Bertrand, 203
Russo-Japanese alliance, 231
    war, 62, 120, 140, 231

Sacasa, 243
St. Bartholomew's Night, 36
St. James, 177
St. John's College, 146
Sepoy Rebellion, 123, 258
Sermon on the Mount, 30
Shakespeare, William, 43
Shaw, Bernard, 203
Shuster, W. Morgan, 103
Sick Man of Europe, 103
Six-power Consortium, 231
Slavery, 108
Solorzano, Carlos, 242
"South Africans, The," Sarah Gertrude Millin, 144-145
South Manchuria Railway, 54
Spanish-American War, 222, 229, 233
Spheres of influence, 117
Stack, Sir Lee, 265
"Stakes of diplomacy," 118
Standard Oil Company, 88, 298
Strike against foreigners in China (1925), 252
    in Nanking (1927), 267
Subject nationalities, 157, 158, 177, 182, 183, 193, 250, 271, 285, 287, 290, 304, 305
Subject nationality, 264

Taft, President, 231
Tammany Hall, 284
Teutonic alliance, 120
Tientsin, Nanking and Shanghai Railway, 56
Timurlane, 21
Tokyo Club, 149
Trans-Siberian Railway, 53

Treaties between United States and Nicaragua, 241-242
    between the United States and Panama, 236
Treaty after Boxer Rebellion, 60
    signed at Washington Conference, 259
    between China and Central Powers, 191
    between Cuba and the United States in regard to sugar, 234
    between Hawaii and the United States (1875), 221
    of Geneva, between Great Britain and Italy, 117
    between United States and Santo Domingo, 237-238
    of Lausanne, 139
    of Nanking of 1842, 47-48
    of Sèvres, 138
    of 1689, Russo-Chinese, 40
    of 1727, Russo-Chinese, 40
    of 1842, and China's tariff, 57
    of Tientsin, 49
    of Vienna, 102
Twain, Mark, "Autobiography," 225

U. S. Marines, 69

Vice-regal Council, 145

Wales, Prince of, 207
War between Italy and Abyssinia, 123-124
    between Turkey and Italy over Tripoli (1911), 121
    of 1763-68, between France and England, 99-100
    of 1856, between England and China, 49

[311]

Wars in China (1842, 1856-60, 1884, 1894, 1900), 123
Washington Conference, 259
Western civilization, 135, 181, 196, 212
  countries, 275
  empires, 253, 300, 304
  expansion, 183
  ideas and forms, 64
  mechanical civilization, 194
  powers, 97, 250, 251, 252, 272
  statesmen, 183
  thought, 131
  world, 79, 129
West, The, 22, 40, 48, 52, 82, 87, 91, 99, 194, 195, 196, 214, 275, 283
White man, aggressions of, 20
  burden of, 16, 21, 71, 99, 130, 225

White man, solidarity of, 183, 185, 191
William, the Conqueror, 34
Wilson, Woodrow, President, 115, 188, 226, 231, 236
Wood, Governor-General, 13, 226, 227, 254
Woolf, Leonard, 142
  "Economic Imperialism," 110
World War, 7, 17, 18, 63, 78, 108, 115, 116, 118, 183, 184, 185, 195, 217, 231, 251, 265

Xavier, St. Francis, 37, 142

Y. M. C. A., 207, 262
Yuan Ming Yuan, palace, 50

Zaghlul Pasha, 265
Zelaya, President, 240

THE
JOHN DAY

ARISE FOR IT IS DAY.

COMPANY
INC.